Dr. Verne's

Northern White Trash Etiquette

Dr. Verne's

Northern White Trash Etiquette

by
Dr. Verne Edstrom, Esq.

toExcel
San Jose New York Lincoln Shanghai

Dr. Verne's Northern White Trash Etiquette

Published by toExcel,
an imprint of iUniverse.com, Inc.

For information address:
iUniverse.com, Inc.
620 North 48th Street
Suite 201
Lincoln, NE 68504-3467
www.iUniverse.com

ISBN: 1-58348-542-2

Printed in the United States of America

To my beloved wife Toni,
who's prettier than a twelver of Grain Belt after
you just unloaded a railroad car

Meet Dr. Verne

How's it going?

The name's Dr. Verne Edstrom, Esq. This here's my book.

You're probably wondering how wholesome Northern White Trash like me got to be a famous book author, hanging around Deep Literary Guys who drink bottled water and don't even own tool belts.

Well, since you asked, this here's the story:

I was born in St. Cloud, Minnesota, which is over by Wisconsin and Canada. Like most decent Northern White Trash, I got a good upbringing.

My ma worked at the quarry and had a sweet AFDC scam going on the side, which taught me good finance at an early age. The old man, he had a union job for about three months when I was six. But mostly he burglarized chicken farms so he could pickle the eggs and sell 'em to bars.

He was a good earner and a good father—until he got shot by Mr. Johansson, who was our neighbor, who wasn't partial to the old man playing hide the power tool with Mrs. Johansson while he was out spear fishing.

The family estate was the envy of St. Cloud. We had a double-wide on 40 acres and more refrigerators on our porch than anybody in town. Some folks might say we was well-to-do.

That's how I got me this prestigious education. I graduated third in my class at the Red Wing Boys Reformatory, which people from them parts will tell you is the Harvard of the Minnesota juvenile correctional system. I also attended the Stillwater State Pen, where I majored in pipe-fitting.

My first wedding was to Alice. I met her while robbing a Denny's one day. You never seen a woman look finer emptying a cash register, her great big hair glistening like a clump of jewels. It looked so sweet I figured it might be worth something at the pawn shop. Problem was, I couldn't get it unattached from her head.

As it turns out, me and Alice got to sparking and next thing you know we's married with four or six kids—I can't remember which.

But then Alice run off with my brother Hal, who only got one ear cuz the other got bit off by a Northern Pike in an ice fishing accident. I figured Alice felt sorry for him. That's why I only tried to shoot Hal once.

Then I got married to Karicia, who got a bad name but a good body. She was what you call your performing artist. Guys still remember her show over at the Palomino Club. She could do some amazing things with a plate of mixed vegetables.

Karicia wasn't partial to having no kids, which is why we only ended up with three. But then I caught her with this guy Sammy in the Palomino men's room. I was pissed, seeing as how he wasn't even kin. So's I smacked Sammy with a towel dispenser.

Well, the blood got to flowing and Karicia got to squealing like a lawyer with a scraped knee. So I went home, grabbed the young ones, and headed for Bemidji, which is known near and far as the World Headquarters of the Northern White Trash Nation.

As you probably know, Bemidji is a fine place to raise kids. There ain't no jobs, which means you can stay on unemployment without them social workers squawking at you. It also got a lot of good places to rob, since most people got power tools.

Me and the kids, we was living in paradise.

◆ THE SECOND FOREWORD ◆

(On account of we couldn't afford all the first so we had to put this one on layaway)

Anyways, I raised them kids right. Taught 'em all my worldly knowledge, like how to hotwire snowmobiles and poach deer.

By junior high, they already had their own scam selling my used Hustlers to fifth graders for fifteen bucks a pop. You might they was born entrepreneurs.

But then I got to figuring the kids needed one of them feminine presences around, someone to teach 'em the fineries of life, such as how to cook a decent pot pie. So I got hitched to Marcie.

If a guy was being charitable, you could say Marcie is a fine looking woman—kind of a female Louie Anderson, only with more facial hair.

But me being the sensitive, nurturing kind, I can say with a true heart that it wasn't looks I was after.

Nope, I first got to sparking with Marcie when I seen her win the wood splitting contest at Lumberjack Days.

She had the muscles of a beer truck driver. Which meant I could branch out into stealing sofas, on account of them hide-a-beds is damn heavy, so you need a partner with decent pipes.

Marcie was a Christian woman. She never used the Lord's name in vain unless she was drunk or shot herself with a nail gun. But she wasn't partial to my thieving ways.

So we up and moved to St. Paul, where the jobs was good. I got me work handling cargo at the airport.

It wasn't a bad job—outside of the actual work. I was making union money and got free steel-toes. It was also good for stealing luggage. (If there's anybody out there needing a set of them Corinthian leather Samsonites with the fruity wheels on the bottom, give me a call.)

But like most decent Northern Trash, me and jobs ain't a good mix. I got what you call disillusioned, which is fancy talk for saying the job sucked. I wanted more from life than dropping computer shipments and stealing suitcases. I wanted some of that enrichment and reward, like they're always talking about on infomercials.

So I did what any God-fearing Northern White Trash would do: I faked a back injury.

Soon I was dipping my beak in that sweet nectar of workers' comp. I convinced the old lady we should move back to Bemidji, where the fishing was better and the insurance guys wouldn't try to videotape me a butchering moose when I was supposed to be laid up.

But like they say in them Hallmark cards, "Life has a way of sticking a shiv in your gut sometimes." Next thing you know, them pointy-heads from the state says I gotta join one of them retraining programs.

So I got to enrolling in the Northern White Trash Studies doctorate program at Bemidji State University. Eleven years later, out comes Dr. Verne Edstrom, Esq.

To tell you the truth, I still don't know what that Esq. stands for.

Now most folks think writing is girlie work, on account of it don't call for the use of power augers. Me, I figured it'd be cake. Instead of hard-ass foremen, they got these dainty editors, who's always rubbing their chins and trying to look deep, like them naked statues in front of libraries. If I was to spend an evening with my good friend Mr. Jim Beam, then show up late the next day, what was they gonna do about it? Choke me with their suspenders?

Down in Des Moines, there was this sissy newspaper called Cityview. They was squawking about their affirmative action, seeing as how they had lots of guys with Caesar hairdos and nose rings, but no decent white trash.

So they give me this column called *Dr. Verne's Northern White Trash Etiquette*. It works like this: Morons write me letters about how they got problems. Then I offer scientific advice, which I mostly just make up. It provides what you call your valuable service.

See, most white trash self-help is geared for them Southerners, who's the lesser of the white trash species. They need basic self-help, like how to operate a can opener or ways to make their 11-year-old cousin unpregnant.

The Northern Trash is more refined. We got union jobs and don't sleep with immediate family. We can hold our liquor and hardly ever shoot each other unless it's important. We need more sophisticated advice, like tips on scamming bookies or who we should kidnap if we're aiming to impress a woman.

Problem is, the decent Northern White Trash wasn't getting no self-help. I wanted to give something back to the community. Which is how I got me this book.

If you ain't buying that explanation, here's a better one: I got eight or ten kids. Seeing as how Marcie's built like a longshoreman, the smart money says she's good for a half-dozen more. So if you don't buy my book, I don't get no money, which means eight to ten kids is gonna be loose on the streets, stealing your car stereo.

And any moron knows a book is cheaper than a car stereo. That's just good financial thinking.

Dr. Verne Edstrom
Des Moines, Iowa

◆ ACKNOWLEDGEMENTS ◆

Special thanks to the following people for helping to make this book not suck that bad:

Little Billy Day, Grandma Bunches Edgington, Davey "138 lbs. of Twisted Steel" Martin, John Shors The Sequel, Z-Man Zurowski, The Macker, Jennifer "Buns of Treated Lumber" Wilson, Big Pipes Kuz and Brenda "You Want A Piece of Me?" Fullick. I'd say gushing stuff about these folks, but it wouldn't be manly.

Also thanks to Pauly Gates for the cover photos, and Roderick Kabel for the cover design. Makes it look like the kinda fancy %$#& they sell in France, don't it?

Finally, thanks to Cityview, Business Publications Corp. and Boss of All Bosses Connie Wimer, for giving me a job so's I could cut back on my burglaries to spend more quality time watching hockey on satellite.

◈ Editor's Note ◈

All letters in this book are real. Some locations have been changed to protect the writers from bill collectors, parole officers, ex-husbands and the guy who's chainsaw they borrowed and never brought back.

◆ TABLE OF CONTENTS ◆

1

SAVE THE WHITE TRASH:
AN INFOMERCIAL

Announcer: The following is paid programming.

The Scene: *A trailer home sits on the edge of the woods with a two-tone paint job—rust and white. The gravel yard is covered with broken toys, a collapsed swingset and a collection of used snowmobiles with a sign that reads, "4 Sell Buy At You's Own Risk." A couple of teenage girls let loose with a 12-gauge on a squirrel hiding beneath a propane tank. A child cries on the front steps. Two men clank under the hood of a International Harvester pickup, cussing their lack of a decent supply of beer.*

Opening monologue, Sally Struthers: *(Enters scene left. Stands before camera, pleading look in her eyes.)* As we speak, an entire culture is vanishing before our eyes. A once-proud people are being stripped of their identity, their way of life. I speak not of the starving children of Africa, nor the oppressed of Central America, who've pretty much tapped out their charitable appeal. No, this crisis is even more insidious. And it's happening right here in America.

(Sitting down next to wailing girl) This child is indicative of the decline of Northern White Trash culture. There was a time when her people represented the backbone of this land. They chopped the wood, hunted the varmints, built the automobiles, filled the prisons. Then everything changed.

(Puts comforting arm around girl. Kid smacks her in the face and runs into house. Flustered, Sally walks toward the truck and stands near the men, who eye her quizzically, wondering what the hell Sally Struthers is doing with a camera crew in their front yard.)

Men like these used to have well-paying jobs. They could afford to buy new trucks with gun racks, and always provided for their families, keeping the cupboards filled with white bread and Jell-O. But then unfeeling corporations moved their factories to Mexico. The Northern White Trash lost their economic self-sufficiency.

First Man: *(Looking up from under hood)* Hey, Sally, you wouldn't happen to have any cigs, would you?

Second Man: *(Chiming in)* You want to get some brewskis, Sally? I'll fly if you buy?

Struthers: *(Ignoring men)* But this wasn't the worst of it. Just ask Dr. Gunder Janke, director of the Institute of Northern White Trash Studies at Bemidji State University.

(Janke enters scene from right, dressed in tweed coat with elbow patches, pissed about the mud he's getting on his shoes.)

Struthers: *(Doing her best to look agonized)* Dr. Janke has spent decades studying the Northern White Trash.

Doctor, what is pushing these people to the brink of extinction?

Janke: *(Puffing on a pipe in an attempt to look professorial)* Well, Sally, there are deep sociological factors at work here.

Struthers: *(Trying to hold back tears)* Like what, Doctor?

Janke: One word, Sally: Fashion. Over the last 20 years popular fashion has appropriated the sacred icons of Northern White Trash culture, stripping away their dignity and pride.

It started when the Punk Movement stole the Northern White Trash concept of messed up hair. For many generations, the Northern White Trash came by this through a penchant for wearing hats all the time and not being particularly concerned with personal hygiene.

Struthers: That's awful. *(Turns away from camera. A tear runs down her cheek.)*

Janke: It gets worse, Sally. Leather jackets, army coats, jackboots—these too were cultural, if not spiritual, icons of the Northern White Trash. All were pirated by popular fashion, leaving the White Trash with a pervasive sense of violation. To put it into perspective, the Northern White Trash are the emotional descendants of Native Americans.

Struthers: My God! *(Moves to all-out sobbing)*

Janke: *(Stepping aside so Struthers' tears don't soil his suit)* That's not all, Sally. A sociological phenomenon known as the Grunge Movement purloined flannel shirts under the guise of popular fashion. As you may know, the Northern White Trash People hold flannel as sacred to their essential being. Yet everyday young men named Bif from Seattle—who couldn't operate a chainsaw if their ma was dying—are desecrating this spiritual value by wearing flannel.

Struthers: *(Near hysteria)* Oh, my Jesus! What will happen to these poor creatures? *(Falls to her knees, weeping uncontrollably.)*

Janke: Well, Sally, it's my considered opinion that it will completely obliterate the Northern White Trash, resulting in their inability to fight, cuss, reproduce, engage in domestic squabbles and drink way too much whiskey. In short: A way of life will be lost forever unless the people watching this show are willing to donate—

Second Man: *(Butting in front of camera)* Hey, Sally, what about them brewskis? A couple a beers would probably get you over what it is you're bawling about.

Struthers: *(Composing herself, she pushes the man from camera view. Mascara is smushed across her face, leaving the impression that she may be a relative of Marilyn Manson.)* That's right, Dr. Janke. We can save these poor creatures if we all just open our hearts.

(Walking toward camera for close-up) If each of you watching this show could give just $5 a day, the Northern White Trash would be saved from extinction.

(The camera pans back. Children suddenly gather around Sally, staring at the camera with sunken eyes.)

By giving just five lousy bucks a day, these children would have the basic necessities of life, like potato chips and satellite TV. And their parents would have plenty of beer, cigs and ammo, thus preserving the Northern White

Trash way of life, so we all may continue to appreciate it for generations to come.

(Return to close-up shot. Sally does Excessively Caring Look.) So give now, and give generously. These children are counting on you.

(Sally turns to hug each child as voice-over begins. Kids rifle through her purse while she's not looking. Camera moves away.)

Announcer: You can help Sally save the Northern White Trash with your contribution. Just send five bucks in unmarked bills to: Save The White Trash, c/o Sally's House, P.O. Box 8423, Beverly Hills, CA 90210.

In return, you'll receive fake pictures of the Northern White Trash you're assisting, along with computer-generated form letters informing you of their progress.

2

REALLY, EUNICE, I THOUGHT THAT DOG WAS A MINNOW

Dear Dr. Verne:

My wife finally flipped. She went out and bought one of them high dollar fluffy yip dogs. You know, the kind you use to clean out your shotgun? Now I know what you're thinking: "Why don't you just be a man and put your foot down, you big sissy?" But ya see, Verne, Eunice is one fine piece of woman. When this woman wears spandex, there isn't one man who don't turn his head. So I needs to know how to tell her that the dog has to go diplomatic like

—*Bob in Quincy*

Dear Bob:

You don't got to tell me Eunice is stepping dynamite. I seen her do karaoke at the Viking Lounge before. If it wasn't for that big scar on her cheek, she could get a job at Hooters.

But women is funny about them fufu dogs. I don't know how you're gonna tell her it's either you or the dog—without you being the one staying at Motel 6.

Me, I'd lie.

Now most self-help guys will tell you lying ain't good. But they ain't married to Eunice.

My advice is to take the dog hunting and leave it out in a field, then tell your woman he ran away. If that don't work—seeing as how fluff dogs ain't easy to drag outta the car—then I'd use it for walleye bait. Just tell Eunice you mistaked it for a large minnow and that you're terribly sorry and that's why you bought her this German shepherd to make up for it.

As I recall, Eunice may be USDA-inspected Grade A meat, but she ain't no master mechanic upstairs

3

How to Know if You're Decent Northern Trash

What you're looking at is one of them scientific tests to make sure you ain't one of The Cell Phone People. It was invented by authentic pointy-heads with initials after their names, so you know it's good.

Check your score at the end. If you gotta get somebody to read it for you, add two points.

1. What makes you and your old man fight the most?

A.) When you catch him tom-catting with the lady from apartment 314, who got a better mustache than Tom Selleck.

B.) When he leaves the toilet seat up, and the kids start using it as a swimming pool.

C.) When he forgets to tape the strongman competition on ESPN while you're working the graveyard shift.

2. Yuppies is good for:

A.) Charging $17,000 for a new tranny on their Acura, on account of they don't know better.

B.) Chopping up and selling for bait on the pier.

C.) When you run out of clay pigeons.

3. What's the most important thing to teach your kids?

A.) How to read so they can understand the racing form.

B.) Chemistry, just in case they need to make pipe bombs sometime.

C.) Math. Cuz that's the lie you always use during parent-teacher conferences.

4. What's the most important thing to look for in a fourth husband?

A.) He's gotta be good in bed, so you'll have something to do when the TV gets repossessed.

B.) He's gotta have a job, or at least a good personal injury case going.

C.) He's gotta be handy with a nail gun, just in case your bookie comes around looking for the money you owe him.

5. What's the most important thing to look for in a fourth wife?

A.) She's gotta know not to talk when the Bengals is on.

B.) Her butt's gotta be small enough to fit in a movie theater seat.

C.) She's gotta be good at lying to the bill collectors, on account of you shouldn't have to do all the damn work around here.

6. Which old country did your ancestors came from?

A.) Greece.

B.) Youngstown.

C.) The Greyhound terminal.

7. Your kid takes a small helping for supper. Do you:

A.) Question his sexual preference.

B.) Search his room to see if he's buying cologne, too.

C.) Tell him to eat up, on account of you ain't raising him to be no supermodel.

8. If you was to win a free vacation from the door-to-door vacuum cleaner salesman, and you could go anywhere, which place would you get your ass to?

A.) Germany, cuz they got a good supply of beer.

B.) Palm Springs, cuz there's lots of old rich people who's easy to mug.

C.) Branson, cuz the old lady loves that Tony Orlando, which means she'll cut you some slack the next time she catches you with her sister behind the dumpster.

9. Say one of your trees falls on the neighbor's yard. You and him got a beef over who should clean it up. Do you:

A.) Forget about it. He never used the part of his house that got crushed anyways.

B.) Shoot him. It ain't polite manners that he's bothering you during the TNT Clint Eastwood marathon.

C.) Tell him he owes you $200, on account of that tree's worth a lotta lumber, then sue 'em when he don't pay.

10. You get a call from the school counselor. Your kid got in a fight. Your first response is:

A.) "Unless you can prove the kid's mine, quit calling."

B.) "You wanna buy some night crawlers?"

C.) "Don't worry. He's just coming down from a meth bender."

11. Your sixteen-year-old daughter tells you she's pregnant. Do you:

A.) Tell her it's about time.

B.) Do the loving parent thing and let her put it on your tab at Planned Parenthood.

C.) Tell her she's gotta move out. She's an adult now and should get her own damned AFDC scam.

12. You just won the lottery. Do you:

A.) Hire one of them pointy-heads with the oval-shaped glasses to invest it wisely.

B.) Pay off your delinquent child support, which will leave enough for a carton of Winstons.

C.) Blow it on slot machines, Jim Beam and chicken, like a decent American.

13. You just got sentenced to eighteen months for your third drunk driving. Now is a good time to:

A.) Stab somebody, on account of the food ain't bad here and you'll get to stay longer.

B.) Turn your life over to God. Maybe He'll pay your lawyer bill.

C.) Sweet talk that lady guard. She's making union money and probably got a nice house with shag carpet and them matador paintings. It'd be a good place for laying on the couch once you get paroled.

14. You're out on your first date with the cute guy from the loading dock. He asks what you want to drink. Do you:

A.) Order one of them top-shelf liqueurs. A man's attractiveness is directly related to how much loot he's willing to blow on you.

B.) Only order a double-shot of Wild Turkey, cuz you wanna seem lady-like.

C.) Order Diet Pepsi. It'll be easier to get yourself knocked up if he don't think you're gonna turn into John Goodman once you get hitched.

15. The landlord calls about the rent being late. Pick the proper Northern White Trash response:

A.) "My deepest apologies. I will inform the trust fund administrator at once."

B.) "Aw, $#@&. My mailman musta got cut down in one of them postal shootings again."

C.) "What &%$#@$#% rent check? I paid you cash two months ago when I hit on the Fireball machine at the Indian casino! Are you trying to %$#@ me here? I got witnesses, mother%$#@$%! You want a piece of me?"

16. If you could shack up with any movie star, who would it be?

A.) Burt Reynolds, on account of you thought he was hot in *Smoky and the Bandit*.

B.) Hugh Grant. He talks funny. Your kids could take him to Show & Tell.

C.) Robert Duvall, on account of he's handsome like Steve Buscemi, but he played a Mafia guy in *The Godfather*, so's he could probably get you a five-finger discount on a camcorder.

17. You're short on jack for Christmas and need to do a quick robbery. Do you?

A.) Mug a FedEx guy. You might score something big, like the payroll checks from a Hardees.

B.) Rob a deli. You haven't done one for a couple weeks, and the Job Corps counselor is always saying how you should keep your skills fresh.

C.) Rob a veterinarian. The kids always wanted a half-pound of horse tranquilizers for Christmas.

18. You dug a septic tank for this guy from work last summer, but he ain't paid up. What's the Northern White Trash way of handling the situation?

A.) Set his house on fire, but don't forget to bring the marshmallows.

B.) Let your dog chew on him, on account of he's cheaper than Purina.

C.) Offer to trade the unpaid bill for that seventy-eight pound sturgeon he got mounted on his wall. It'll make for good bragging when the in-laws come over.

19. It's you and your woman's tenth anniversary (if you don't count the time she was shacking up with that trucker from Ohio). You wanna do something classy. Do you:

A.) Give her your leftover KFC from lunch.

B.) Steal some flowers from a rich lady's lawn, then have your buddy deliver 'em so it looks like you paid top dollar.

C.) Make her a nice Swanson's dinner and put on the Pirates game, then let her sit in the good recliner tonight—just so she don't make a habit of it.

20. It's Saturday night. Your old man's got the annual Ducks Unlimited banquet. But you're playing third base for Len's Bar in the state softball regionals. Problem is, you got no babysitter for the three youngest. Do you:

A.) Make the old man take 'em to the banquet. The kids gotta learn to drink sometime.

B.) Let 'em stay home by themselves. This is what shrinks call nurturing their independence.

C.) Put 'em in foster care. Your folks did it to you, and you ain't turned out so bad.

Correct answers:

1. C; 2. B; 3. A; 4. B; 5. C; 6. C; 7. B; 8. C; 9. A; 10. B; 11. A; 12. C; 13. C; 14. A; 15. C; 16. C; 17. B; 18. A; 19. C; 20. C

Rating your score:

18-20: You're authentic Northern White Trash. Get to breeding ASAP. America needs more people like you.

15-17: You're pretty good trash, but went a little fruity after that time you put designer mustard on your ballpark dog. Take a chainsaw to your foreman's car. You'll feel better.

10-14: You're a half-breed: part trash, part Cell Phone People. You're pretty handy with a circular saw, but your last brawl was in junior high, when you gave up after someone named Chad ripped a button off your best shirt.

5-9: Nobody'd want you on their dart team. You're always squawking about second-hand smoke. You run like a girl.

1-5: Drive your car into a bridge pylon.

4

GREAT MORAL QUESTIONS ON WHAT'S MANLY & WHAT AIN'T

Newlywed varmint storage problems

Dear Dr. Verne:

Each winter my friend Jeff has been trapping coon and storing them in the freezer until he had enough to sell. (The buyer don't want Jeff skinnin' 'em 'cause he ain't very good at it.) Now that Jeff got married, things changed.

His wife spotted a frozen paw sticking out of a garbage bag and resting on a leftover wedding cake she'd saved. She made him remove the coons and then she threw out the cake.

Jeff can't store the coons outside 'cause the dogs eat them, or it warms up too much and they bloat. His mom lives down the road and lets him use her freezer, but it's a small one and filled up fast. He even asked me if I got any extra fridge space.

Seems to me he ought to solve this problem back home instead of shipping coons out across the county. What's your thoughts on this?

—*Concerned on the Mesabi Range*

Dear Mesabi Range Guy:

Jeff gotta lay down the law, only it ain't as easy as it used to be.

Back in the old days, a guy could tell his woman how it was gonna be, and she'd listen. Hell if I know why. It just was.

But now they got this marital equality. That means you got what they call shared responsibilities, which is the fruity way of saying men don't got it good no more.

Me, I ain't exactly partial to it, on account of in the old days all we had to do is howl and drink and forget to pick stuff up from the grocery store. Why be a moron and give that up?

But under this shared responsibility, you gotta divide the bossing evenly.

Take Jeff's wife. She oughtta be in charge of cooking, cleaning, and tending after the kids and money, on account of women don't drink up paychecks as much.

Jeff, he should be boss of fixing stuff, shooting at the stray pit bulls and saying where the dead coons is stored.

Problem is, Jeff's wife is probably one of them feminisms who gone to college. She's looking to get say over the freezer, too, so she can expand her sphere of influence, which is military talk for saying Jeff's about to get his ass kicked.

That's why most decent trash get a little something going on the side. Business guys call this finding an auxiliary supplier. If Jeff was to score himself a side honey— I hear there's a woman at the Mountain Iron bait shop who's loose—then he'd also score an extra coon storing facility.

But what I'm really thinking about is that wedding cake. You know where Jeff's old lady tossed it? I wouldn't mind you sending me a piece if you could find it.

Captured by the yuppies

Yo Verne, You Dawg:

We need help. One of our buds got drug to the suburbs by his ol' lady. Better than his ol' double-wide, she said.

We've been worried about him, but he's trying to make it right by not tying his sweaters around his neck and trading his wuss Isuzu Trooper for an F-150 4x4 extended cab. He keeps making noises 'bout putting a dirty mattress, a couple of buckets of the Colonel's extra greasy and nine or ten twelvers of Busch in the back for partying with the girls from Big Earl's strip joint.

But when push comes to shove, he keeps drinking Zima and talking about racquetball.

What can we do to help 'em get back on the Beam and not get us in jail or shot by his woman?

—*Bob & Ray,*
Windsor, Ontario

Dear Fellas:

You gotta get him divorced, which ain't as hard as it sounds.

See, them yuppies is always trading in their used wives. Say they marry a babe, but she gets to having kids and eating too much of them quiches. Next thing you know, their woman's the size of a decent strong safety.

Now good white trash knows there ain't nothing wrong with a woman who got a little beef on her, specially if she's handy with a post hole digger. Hell, if God wanted women to be perfect, he wouldda made 'em into bass boats instead.

But them yuppies don't like ladies who got worn tread, on account of it don't impress nobody at the company summer golf outing.

Since your buddy is probably already brainwashed into them fruity suburb ways, tell him his old lady's getting craggy and the neighbors been talking about how she's better fit for a sheep farm. He'll dump her like a bad slice of ham.

But since she got all the loot, the guy'll be sleeping on your couch in no time. Then you can hook him to a decent lady, the kind who got big hair and puts on her makeup with a fire hose. Once he gets in the ever-loving arms of some fine Northern White Trash, consider the guy cured.

Dockers Anonymous

Dear Dr. Verne:

I think of myself as kind of a regular guy. I drive a pickup, drink domestic beer straight out of the can, wear boots and ain't never used any of that sissy sunscreen. I got one problem: I wear Dockers trousers. Not the kind with the fruity pleats, but dang if they're still Dockers and I got to put 'em on every day. Is there a support group like Dockers Anonymous or some head shrinker that can help me?

P.S. I ain't no sissy lawyer or nothing like that.

—Mike in Billings

Dear Mike:

Wearing Dockers is one of the Original Sins, right up there with punching grandmas and singing along with the

Spice Girls on the radio. I'd be damn sure I wasn't outside when it's lightning out. Three-to-one says God smokes your ass before I get done with this here response.

See, everybody knows Dockers guys is kin to Liberace. In the commercials, they're never talking about venison sausage or Skoal or repacking the bearings on a '82 Trans Am. They're always saying dainty stuff like, "My, that's a nice blouse you got on."

I'm thinking you need medical attention. Back when I was young, if I was to ever act fruity—like maybe watch public TV—Verne Sr. would take me out back and pound my ass with a Webber grill.

This is what medical guys call your Pavlovian experience. Anytime you go fruity, like say the words "trousers" or "pleats," one of your buddies should smack you with a grill. Take it from me: A guy gets to learning fast this way, specially if it's loaded up with lighter fluid.

My old man's gone sissy

Dear Dr. Verne:

I'm 16 and I got a problem. It's my old man. I mean, he's cool enough, was a grunt in 'Nam and rolls his own ammo for his .44 mag.

The trouble is his job. He's a registered nurse. I got in so many fights about it in school I got expelled. I keep begging him to get a manly job, like loading trucks at the co-op or faking a back injury in a fight with a psych patient and go on disability.

But he just tells me to shut up and be glad he can afford my Ritalin. How can I deal with this, Doc?

—Ike in Minot

Dear Ike:

If the old man keeps registered nursing, sooner or later he's bound to buy a Range Rover, just so's he can get a good parking place at the Nordstroms sale. He's gonna forget how to cuss. And you'll know he's on the brink of lesbianism when he starts hyphenating his last name and trying to order big salads at Long John Silvers.

What you gotta do is appeal to the old man's heart. Let him know that you care too much to see him go wussified, that if he don't quit that damn registered nursing, God'll send him to the dainty part of Hell, where they only serve Coors Light and the big screens all show figure skating.

The White Zinfandel Crisis

Dear Dr. Verne:

Last weekend, on the promise of getting a Texas fifth of Jack, I helped my worthless brother-in-law replace the tranny in his candy red '72 Nova. Later that day, he came over and gave me a sixer of light beer and something called White Zinfandel (only it wasn't white, it was sissy pink). I yelled at him, told him to never come back. Was I right to act this way? Should I have accepted the light beer and wine? I assume they got alcohol in them.

—*Clyde in Bangor*

Dear Clyde:

Yeah, they got alcohol in 'em, but only enough to get a computer geek hammered. And most folks say if you drink 'em, you'll go weird and start talking about Julie Andrews movies.

See, if you're in a bar, and you're ordering light beer, you might as well be saying, "I enjoy wearing women's undergarments and could you please turn the big screen to soccer." I could go on about what you call your sociological implications, but the short of it is, light beer's for guys who cried during *Sleepless in Seattle.*

As for the Zinfandel, it's obviously Europe-sounding, where nobody can even clean their own fish, much less do a decent Pizza Hut robbery.

I'm figuring you gotta get this guy away from your sister, before they get to reproducing. The guy probably can't even punch out an interior decorator. You don't want your nephew getting no poor role modeling.

Scumbag lawyer: 'Babes won't listen to me'

Dear Dr. Verne:

I need your help. I am an attorney in Orchard Park, NY. There are three women in my life who are making it a living hell: my secretary, who does what she wants when she wants; my colleague, who criticizes everything I do; and my wife, who only lets me have some once in a blue moon.

How can I get these women to do what I want?

—*PW'd in Orchard Park*

Dear Candy-Ass Lawyer:

A course no woman gonna pay you respect. You're a lawyer, for chrissakes.

Let me ask you this: Say you got a friend who got this dainty-ass job, right? And say all this guy does for a living is lie, throw paperwork at people and wear overpriced suits made by some guy who drinks Chardonnay and don't even like beer nuts? Would you A.) Respect him, or B.) Beat him with a roll of duct tape?

Your secretary don't listen to you cuz she don't have to. What you gonna do about it? Hair spray her?

Same goes for your wife. Most lawyers got pipes like Japanese businessmen. What you gonna say? "If you sleep with me honey I'll show you my dayplanner?" Just be thankful she ain't sold your ass to one of them animal testing labs.

Now about this colleague. I don't know what the hell you're talking about, but it sounds like pervert talk. You ain't one of them creeps who collects pictures of naked children, is you?

I'm thinking you need what you call your intensive therapy. First off, you gotta quit that fruity job. On the manly scale, it's like being a poetry professor.

Second off, lose the cute little Tommy Hilfiger uniforms you probably wear in your off time. The only ladies that stuff attracts is them fancy ones with the smiles so tight they look like they're held up by four-inch sheet metal screws. Buy yourself something classy instead, like a couple of Bruce Smith jerseys.

Then you gotta get manly in your talking. Me, I'd start out by practicing some basic manly phrases like, "Woman, you got more of that roast beef?" or "I wonder what a DNR permit costs for hunting Pauly Shore."

Then you gotta trade in your briefcase for a tool belt. Since you probably still walk prissy, I'd stick something big in it just to compensate, like maybe a shop vac.

Finally, I'd weld me a wench and a blade on the front of your Nissan Pathfinder so it don't look like all you haul is them Waterford crystals. If you got no blade, just cut the metal outta your neighbor's tool shed when it's dark out, then brace it with some treated four-by-fours. She ain't gonna look pretty, but the ladies is gonna think you got more chest hairs.

5

THE NORTHERN WHITE TRASH 10 COMMANDMENTS

1. You shall have no other Gods before me—except for cable TV.

2. You shall not make any carved image of Heaven above, cuz God owns the merchandising rights. Don't try horning in on His turf or He'll beat your ass with pool cue.

3. You shall not take the Lord's name in vain, unless it involves bosses, congressmen, the Dallas Cowboys or shooting yourself in the spleen while you're out pheasant hunting.

4. Remember the Sabbath day, keep it holy. If God wanted you to work, he would have made football on Tuesdays.

5. Honor your father and mother, cuz someday they're gonna croak. You could inherit yourself their F-150 if you stop acting like an ingrate.

6. You shall not commit murder, except when there's a good reason, like finding your old man in bed with a 16-year-old cashier from the Dairy Queen.

7. You shall not commit adultery. Okay, just don't do it at the motel where your sister-in-law works.

8. You shall not steal. (Only applies in Utah and Canada.)

9. You shall not bear false witness against your neighbor, unless you figure he's gonna rat you out on that bowling alley robbery you did. Then beat him to the punch.

10. You shall not covet your neighbor's house, nor shall you covet your neighbor's wife, especially if he's about to get released on parole. Then again, if he's doing time for something sissy like embezzling from a flower shop, covet all you want.

6

THE MANLY MAN'S GUIDE TO VEHICLES: A SCIENTIFIC STUDY

Priests will tell you that man was started by Adam, that moron from the Garden of Eden.

I ain't buying.

First off, a guy who orders an apple instead of steak ain't smart enough to start a civilization. Hell, they hadn't even invented cash registers yet. What's he ordering a Granny Smith when the ribeyes was free?

Second off, judging by the way men think about vehicles, the smart money's giving 12-to-1 that man evolved from apes or Trent Lott.

See, most men think all they gotta do is get a sweet machine, and the ladies'll be flopping around 'em like a herd of gooses. Ain't so.

This ain't to say your vehicle selection don't got consequences. Fact is, for lesser white trash, a decent machine is the only thing keeping you from reading *Men's Health*.

But them sociologists is always saying vehicles is an extension of ourselves. I don't know what that means. Which is why I got me this scientific survey.

It's for finding out what vehicles is decent and manly, and what is for The Cell Phone People. The survey was done very scientific-like, which means we didn't do no shots till the interviewing was over.

You got a problem with that?

Pickups

Pickup trucks obviously offer the manliest in driving experiences. Personally, Dr. Verne is a Ford man. But you gotta like that Dodge Ram. It got a hood the size of a rich man's tool shed, and it's named after an animal that head-butts stuff.

But the fact is, there ain't no going wrong with a full-size pickup—unless it's made by them Japanese, who suck at hockey—or the bed's so clean you could iron Sunday dresses on it.

That ain't true about midget pickups. According to that science I was telling you about, ninety-eight percent of 'em is driven by fitness instructors. Seventy-two percent never caught a fish heavier than a box of Kleenex. And 113 percent think NASCAR is that country by Egypt.

Station Wagons

The most underrated vehicle.

First off, they pass the No. 1 test for determining a decent white trash machine: They can haul plywood.

Second off, they'll score you sympathy points. Most people figure a guy driving a wagon collects ceramic cats. Either way, that makes you invisible, leaving you free to drunk drive and haul oversized loads of sheet metal.

When a cop sees a sports utility vehicle swerving on the road, he usually says, "That man is compensating for a very small penis and is probably snorting coke. Let's pull him over, Mel."

But when a cop sees a swerving station wagon, he says, "Poor schmuck. His wife probably jacked him in the divorce and all he can afford is a damned station wagon. Whattaya say we let this one go, Mel?"

I once had a wagon with a rusted out floor board so you could dump your empties along the freeway for the bums to pick up. That's why station wagons is also good for community service.

Luxury Vehicles

A lotta people don't figure white trash got luxury cars. But say you done good in the scrap business, and you're fixing to buy your woman something nice. For my money, there ain't no better machine than the Lincoln.

First off, Lincolns is named after a famous president with a good beard, which means he could probably hunt muskrat. And let it be said that the Lincoln is the finest bar-hopping machine on Earth. If your pal Joey starts ralphing in the back, you can roll down the power windows from the driver's seat so's he don't get it on the carpet. It's got a big trunk, which is good if you're gonna kidnap your ex-girlfriend's dog. And you can rent the back seat out to your buddies in case they wanna get lucky in the bar parking lot.

Minivans

Minivans is kind of like station wagons: They get a bad rap even though they can haul plywood.

The upside is minivans got good kid hauling powers, and can carry a decent amount of saw horses or sheet rock if you're into burglarizing garages.

Problem is, eighty-three percent of people figure if you own a minivan, you probably shouldda just dumped the wife and kids and paid child support instead, on account of it's cheaper. Which makes you one of them fiscally irresponsibles. Which is why you shouldn't buy no goddamned minivan.

Wimp Vehicles

Wimp cars is them cigar boxes with wheels that got names like Altima or Estrogen. Most people get to figuring wimp cars is for hairdressers and environmentalists. Which they is.

They don't got good clearance when you're ditch driving and get wrecked up easy when you get hammered and hit the neighbor's garage.

However, eighty-nine percent said if you was to put a brush guard on, even an Escort would look cool. They're also good for ramming Mercedes when you're jousting for the last parking spot at the Broncos game.

Sports Cars

Old Verne got a serious beef about sports cars.

Okay, so there ain't nothing finer than a babe with one of them top-shelf peroxide jobs, driving down the freeway with the wind in her big hair, looking like she got a thick, blonde tumbleweed attached to her head.

That, friends, is good living.

But it ain't so pretty when you see Skippy, cute little executive, shoved into his red sports car from France, driving like Ernie Irvan on crank cuz he's late for his Lamaze class.

Seventy-nine percent of guys with sports cars ain't very good at softball. Eighty-one percent cross picket lines. And 163 percent would be mostly blubber and mush if you was in a plane crash and got stranded and had to eat 'em.

Sport Utility Vehicles

These used to be the preferred vehicle of four out of five white trash. "I drive through highway medians and don't gotta stop if I hit a grocery store." That was the message they sent.

Sport utility vehicles was also good for shining deer and tearing up your girlfriend's yard after she dumped you.

But then the Cell Phone People started buying 'em. Everything went to &%$#.

According to science, eighty-two percent—give or take forty percent—says sports utility vehicles is now for lightweights. The heaviest thing they haul these days is soccer equipment and cappuccino.

Unless you gotta pre-'90s American-made with a classy naked lady hood ornament, the only thing this truck says is, "I can't change my own oil; please pass the Cafe Vienna."

7

TODD'S BIG TORNADO SCAM

Dear Dr. Verne:

During the last tornado at my trailer court, me and my wife Lorlene were only able to get six out of seven of our kids into the culvert. The tornado picked up Travis, our ten-year-old, who was making a run for the woods. The damn thing dropped him in a nearby farmer's sorghum field.

Now this farmer hates me cuz I'm always fishin' his pond without his okay. So he recognizes Travis as my kid and turns him over to the county social services department and starts ranting about child neglect. The local press picked up on it and showed a lot of video of Travis limping around with all these bruises and bandages.

Now, Verne, I know Travis and I know his fake limp. He's milking this for all it's worth. The whole county is treating him like a king.

I'm mighty proud of him. There's even some old rich couple who wants to adopt him. This couple would probably die soon after, and Travis and his real family would be set for life.

My problem is Lorlene misses Travis and wants to fight to get him back. Me, I'm loving the extra room in the trailer and next week I could save $3 when I take the family to the drive-in for our summer vacation.

Verne, what should I do?

—*Todd in Tulsa*

Dear Todd:

You and the missus oughtta be right proud the way you raised your boy. There ain't a lotta kids these days who will milk a leg injury for the sake of their family.

But you gotta do something about the missus, Todd. First off, it's her job to think about what's best for the family. If she'd do one of them cost benefit analysises, which is how rich guys figure stuff out, she'd know it's way better economics to have Travis soaking them elderlies than mooching off you.

Second off, tell her to quit bawling about missing the kid. Hell, he's only ten. She'll have plenty a time to see him when them old folks die, you get rich, and all you gotta do is sit on the porch, swill Beam and watch the drunk drivers ram the train bridge.

Fact is, I ain't seen my two oldest in three years, ever since they got caught trying to rob that dermatologist in Nebraska. But you don't hear my woman squawking. That's because she knows if them two's in prison, they ain't at home snarfing up all the Captain Crunch and liquor.

8

How to Tell if Your Job Sucks

A lot of people have a hard time figuring out what's the best career: working, welfare or workers comp?

Most folks go straight to welfare or workers comp, seeing as how jobs can rarely compete with laying on the couch and watching cable all day. But in its recent report, "Jobs That Don't Suck," the U.S. Department of Commerce discovered there were at least 23 in America.

So how do you know if you got one of 'em? Just answer "yes" or "no" to the following questionnaire. Your job's suckage rating is figured at the bottom.

1. Does your job got free coffee that ain't that limp-wristed kind guys with berets and sandals drink?

2. Can you ash on the floor and set fire to stuff if nobody's using it?

3. Do you get paid time off on major holidays, like Opening Day, St. Patrick's Day and Deer Hunting Season?

4. Is it okay to be drunk some of the time, just so it ain't every day?

5. Does the other employees bring good lunches you can steal outta the company fridge when they ain't looking?

6. Does the boss still fall for the Call-in-a-Bomb-Threat-When-You's-Too-Hung-Over-to-Show-Up-for-Work Scam?

7a. If you're a man, does the women employees wear halter tops and not look like them Russian ladies?

7b. If you're a woman, are the men employees you're having affairs with respectful enough not to call your house when the old man's home?

8. Is there wildlife you can shoot out the window during lunchtime?

9. Is there a bitchy human resource lady who's fun to torture by putting cig burns in her paperwork and telling her, "You look pretty today, kinda like Eva Braun"?

10. Can you make a decent score by busting into the pop machine when no one's looking?

Suckage Rating:

· 8-10: If you answered "yes" to eight or more questions, you're probably in the Lucky 23. That means it ain't a good idea to spray paint cars in the executive parking lot no more.

· 5-7: It's probably worth keeping—if you answered "yes" to question 10 and you're getting at least 50 bucks a week.

· 3-4: What are you, some kind of moron?

· 0-2: Consider yourself excommunicated from the Northern White Trash Nation.

9

WHAT THE &%$# IS A 401(K)?

Dear Dr. Verne:

What the hell is a 401(k)? I've heard the other shop guys talk about it during cig breaks, and I nod my head like I know what they're talking about, but I have no clue. The only thing I know is that I have to decide if I want a little money taken out of my paycheck now so it will pay off later when I'm old.

The whole thing sounds like a great excuse to talk to Becky in the payroll department—she has some bodacious ta-tas—but I want to know what the hell I'm talking about. I don't want to write those newspaper assholes about it because I want my answer in English.

So, Verne, should I sacrifice some cig and Beam money now? Will it really pay off when I retire? Is it true some suit-wearing, bottled-water drinking pussy from New York will have control of my money?

—*Confused in Reno*

Dear Confused:

First off, a 401(k) is basically the same as a savings account, except they call it 401(k) cuz it was named by geek accountants who like giving goofy names to stuff so no one can understand it and you gotta hire their sorry ass.

The good thing about a 401(k) is it gets taken outta your paycheck before you can drink it up. Better yet, your boss, if he ain't a huge cheap-ass like mine, usually kicks in some money, too. This means the boss is actually paying for the Beam you'll be drinking when you retire.

The downside is that you probably ain't never gonna retire, on account of 94 percent of all Northern Trash die from being mistaken for abandoned kitchen appliances and crushed in garbage compactors before they're 65.

The other downside is some candy-ass from New York is gonna be handling your money, which means he might blow it all investing in wine cooler futures. At which point you get some guys together from the union and kick his ass, which would be fun, which means it ain't a complete loss.

10

THE 10 HOTTEST NORTHERN WHITE TRASH CAREER OPPORTUNITIES

Seeing as how them bullet-proof windows hurt the convenience store robbing industry, a lot of Northern Trash been thinking about career changes. Problem is, most of the factory jobs gone to Thailand, which is too far to commute. That's leaving a lot of trash in what you call your state of despair.

But don't go a worrying. There's still a lot of jobs where you hardly have to work—much less show up—that pay better than AFDC.

A look at the Top 10 high growth professions in the 21st Century:

1. CEO

The upside: The hardest thing you're ever gonna do is say, "Have my helicopter ready in 10 minutes." Most of the time you sit around firing people for being too old or pretending to read reports from the Pacific Rim Project. And you always got an excuse for missing work when you get drunk and fall off the porch. Just call your secretary and say, "I'll be at home working on my vision statement today."

The downside: Guys'll expect you to play golf. You gotta get one of them molded plastic executive hairdos. And the ladies at work will wanna talk about mutual funds instead of muscle cars.

The pay: Higher than you can count with an eighth grade public school education. Plus, you get stock options. I don't exactly know what these is, but you ever see a CEO mooching drinks at closing time?

2. Crack Whore

The upside: You can call in sick every day on account of it's part of the job requirements. You don't gotta pay taxes or rent, cuz crack whores figure good living is clean cardboard in an alley behind a laundromat. Plus, you get to travel to exotic places like bus stations.

The downside: No paid vacations. Company headquarters is the bathroom of a Phillips 66.

The pay: None. But since you're keeping expenses low, this is what them granola eaters call living off the fat of the land.

3. Designated Hitter

The upside: Sit on the bench, say uplifting things like, "C'mon, Jonesy, we need a hit," swing a club four times a day, then beeline it to the clubhouse deli spread before your teammates get in and all that's left is the macaroni salad.

The downside: You don't get to play in the field. That means you won't score extra bus fare when the drunks pelt you with quarters at Tiger Stadium.

The pay: We're talking guaranteed contracts of $5 million for five years. Bonus round: Gouge suburban punks for 20 bucks an autograph at baseball card shows.

4. Trophy wife

The upside: Watch TV. Lunch. Watch more TV.

The downside: You're gonna have to marry some dainty guy with Roman numerals after his name. He's gonna buy you exercise equipment, which means if you pound cheese puffs all day, he'll trade you in for a new model that runs on grapefruit and bean sprouts.

The pay: Free Lexus, big screen and makeup. You also get unlimited credit cards to binge shop for halter tops and plastic lawn deer.

5. Third World Dictator

The upside: You can call yourself a general and order aircraft carriers to take your buddies fishing. Live in a palace where they got servants who'll fetch cigs and chocolate milk from the SuperAmerica.

The downside: Everybody's calling you El Presidente, which sounds kinda sissified for the boss of a country. Most Third World gas stations ain't worth robbing. Everybody talks Mexican on cable.

The pay: You own the country. This comes in handy when you're short on gas money.

6. Symphony Violinist

The upside: Hack away with a funny stick on a violin, then pretend the screeching is famous music from Austria. Rich guys pay top dollar to hear this stuff. You only gotta work three-hour shifts. And the boss is some guy who wears white gloves and is always flopping his arms like a mallard with a sore wing, which means you don't gotta follow his orders. What's he gonna do to you? Hit you with his little baton?

The downside: You gotta dress up in a tux. Your relatives is gonna think you're a waiter from them bird food restaurants downtown.

The pay: How am I supposed to know? Get off your ass and find out for yourself. I'm tired of doing all the work here.

7. Bar Hag

The upside: Sit at the bar, sweet talk toothless guys who couldn't buy a decent woman with a profit sharing check, and be ugly.

The downside: Shifts last from 8 a.m. to 4 a.m. You gotta survive on cocktail wieners from happy hour.

The pay: Free drinks. Some nights you get to sleep in the cab of a new Dodge Ram.

8. Congressman

The upside: It's basically the same job as a bar hag: sit around, blab and mooch stuff. Mostly you just eat free steak dinners from lobbyists, go on fact-finding missions to country clubs in Hawaii, and vote to let chemical companies build hazardous waste dumps at pre-schools.

The downside: They cut out your heart as a job requirement. People will watch to make sure you don't steal the silverware when you come over for dinner.

The pay: Six figures plus bribes, junkets, free dinners, sex with interns, and an office full of Ivy League ass-kissers who can haul shingles in case you get a roofing job.

9. Punk Rock Hairdresser

The upside: Change your name to Francois, get a caulking gun, blast their hair with some tub and tile sealer, mess it all up and charge 'em $100 a pop. They're punkers. They'll think it's cutting edge.

The downside: You gotta tell people you're a hairdresser. If you get the urge to arrange flowers, call 911.

The pay: 100 bucks for three minutes of work. Try making that selling plasma.

10. Workers Comp

The upside: It's kind of like being a trophy wife, only without the credit cards or exercise equipment. Just fake a back injury, sit around reading TV Digest, watch fishing shows and have your kids fetch Mountain Dew and Count Chocula.

The downside: You gotta go to the doctor. Sometimes they schedule appointments right in the middle of that Bruins-Islanders rerun you was meaning to watch.

The pay: $400 a month, plus quality time with the kids in front of the TV.

11

WHY HOCKEY IS A BETTER JOB THAN THE MARINES

Dear Dr. Verne:

When I was 16 I dropped out of school so I could get the manliest job I could think of, the U.S. Marine Corps. It was great. They gave me a gun and let me shoot pinko commie bastards for a living. Then on the weekend (when I wasn't kicking butt), me and the boys would go down to Tijuana, get loaded off tequila, beat the &%$# out of some Navy boys and score us some women.

Nowadays I'm lucky if I get to kick ass once a month, seeing as all we do is "peace keeping" missions and they been givin' me wussy paper pushin' geek jobs. What's worse is now they lettin' in women and fruity Zima drinkin' boys who couldn't load a Tow missile if their life depended on it.

I was thinkin' of leaving and joining a militia, but I don't want to leave my old Corps. What should I do?

—*Corps Forever*

Dear Corp:

First thing you gotta do is get a new name. If you're asking me, "Corps" is kinda foreign sounding, like guys at a bar might think you're from Belgium.

But I'm feeling for you, pal. Fact is, the Marines is getting unmanlified. It used to be that decent people like you could make a good living shooting commies, getting hammered and smacking around them Navy fruits. (If they're so manly, how come Navy guys dress like them rich kids in black and white movies?) But you don't wanna join no militia.

Militia guys is Grade A U.S. Inspected Losers who think they're manly by blowing up old people and daycare centers in Oklahoma. You think that candy-ass Tim McVeigh would help you out in a bar fight, or even give you a decent game of quarters? Hell, no. Give that fruity two beers and he'll be barfing and talking about going over to Hitler's apartment to watch cable. You're too manly for hanging out with stiffs who need machine guns to deer hunt.

If you think the Marines is going sissy, join a hockey team. Them boys could drink Marines under the table, you only get a five-minute penalty for brawling, and they let in commies now on account of affirmative action. You can hack 'em with your stick all you want. That's only a two-minute penalty.

Besides, hockey got less rules than Marines and you don't gotta get the bad hairdo that scares away chicks. Plus, you still get summers off to practice up your drinking and fighting.

12

A FINANCIAL PRIMER FOR SCAMMING OUTTA YOUR GAMBLING DEBTS

Ever since the Vikings landed in Ireland and told 'em they was just looking for a decent pancake house, the Northern White Trash has been the world's best liars.

This comes in handy when you gotta scam outta your gambling debts.

After all, gambling involves taking on the three most powerful forces on Earth: your woman, your boss and your bookie.

Let's start with the baddest, the one who can do you the most damage: your woman.

This is where a lotta guys go wrong. They get to figuring, "Hey, I'm the man. I'm the breadwinner here. If I wanna drop fifty bucks on the Wolverines, I'm gonna. A man's gotta be the king of his own row house, otherwise what's the use of having chest hairs?"

Pointy-headed college guys call this "delusional thinking," which is a fancy way of saying you're a dumb ass.

Everybody knows women run the world. Sure, men get all the good jobs, like president and foreman. But women got the power.

Take the president. Say he wants to bomb South Carolina, on account of he's slumping in the polls. But say his woman don't want him to, on account of she don't wanna see no blown up people on TV unless it's a movie.

If he goes ahead and bombs, she ain't making him supper no more. Which means he's gotta eat them convenience store subs with the ham that looks like it was butchered in 1973.

That's why you can't be talking no breadwinner stuff. You gotta finesse the situation. And finesse is French for "lying your ass off."

Let's try ourselves a pop quiz.

Say your woman lets you keep 100 bucks outta each paycheck for everyday stuff, like cigs and gas and crank. But say you lay fifty bucks on Calgary over San Jose.

First off, what the hell you betting on Calgary for? A course you're gonna lose. Which means you'll run out of money before the next payday. Which means you gotta ask your woman for more.

Do you:

A.) Tell her you bet on Calgary and lost again?

B.) Tell her you was robbed, but the guy only took $55 (don't forget the juice) cuz he didn't want to be stealing too much from no family man?

C.) Tell her you happen to run into Father McGarry, and he was saying how they need money for the parish horse shoe league, so you donated $55?

D.) All of the above.

If you answered A, you're about to get a butt whupping. Even your woman knows not to bet on Calgary.

If you answered B, you suck at lying. Either quit betting or get divorced, cuz you ain't gonna be able to do both.

If you answered D, you're good at talking outta your ass. You'd make a good drunk or a senator from Mississippi.

But if you answered C, you're righteous Northern White Trash.

The best way to turn a &%$#up into your advantage is to pretend like you did noble. If you tell your woman you gave the money to Father McGarry, she might be pissed, on account of she thinks Father McGarry is one of them perverts. But she can't be mad too long, on account of women is suckers for doing good deeds.

That means whenever you blow your money, always say something noble, like you bought twenty-five boxes of Girl Scout cookies. Or they got a United Way drive at the plant. Or your girlfriend was short on the rent and you had to front her.

Problem is, pretty soon you gonna run out of noble stuff to say. That means you gotta find an auxiliary loot source.

Enter the boss.

He May Be Evil, But At Least He's Stupid

The Scouting Report:

Raised by yuppies who forced him to play soccer at an early age...Wore lots of matching outfits...Couldn't get a date for the prom...Flunked out of business school...Married a beefy woman named Darlene who whines like a opera singer with multiple gunshot wounds...Bought a red sports car...Failed the real estate exam...Got into bossing to take revenge on the world...

The good thing about bosses is they ain't very smart. You probably didn't know that boss in Swedish means, "Can somebody show me how to run the candy machine?"

Which means you got the advantage.

Say you laid fifty bucks on St. Louis and seven over the Eagles. A course you lost. What were you thinking, going with the Rams?

Problem is, you already spent most of your noble lies on your woman. So you gotta figure out a new batch of noble stuff to tell your boss so he'll front you your paycheck.

Do you:

A.) Tell him bad-ass space guys—way meaner than them guys from *Star Trek*—kidnapped you and forced you to bet on the Rams, on account of they don't know no bookies on Earth?

B.) Tell him you saw some orphans hanging out in the ally behind your house, so's you kicked their ass on account of you figured it was them who stole your jigsaw last week, but then you found out wrong, so's you had to buy 'em fifty-five bucks worth of Jim Beam to make up for it?

C. Tell him your kid is having an esophagus transplant, and you need fifty-five bucks to cover the co-payment?

D. All of the above.

Seeing as how we're talking about the boss, all of 'em will work—at least the first couple of times. But after awhile, he'll be getting to suspiciousness. That's why it's best to lie about stuff they don't understand.

Good lies is stuff like, "My daughter's gotta get her pancreas eradicated" or "My wife's getting a skin graft on her uterus."

He won't know what the hell you're talking about, so he'll have to fork over the money, otherwise the guys at the plant'll be laughing at him more than they already do.

But pretty soon them pointy-heads in accounting will figure you got fronted on your paycheck till next July. They'll cut you off. Which means you need a new batch of lies for Arch-Nemesis No. 3, the bookie.

The Old Rich Uncle From Duluth Trick

This is where the lying gets hard. Bookies is trained professionals. They ain't falling for nothing about pancreases or skin grafting.

Let's look at the situation from his eyes: You bet on Calgary and the Rams; he knows you're a moron. You been mumbling about your wife; he knows you're in deep &%$# at home. And the boys from the plant already told him how you ain't got no paychecks coming till July. That means unless you get to some serious lying, he's gonna cash you in.

Meet the Old Rich Uncle From Duluth Trick.

Tell your bookie you ain't got money this week on account of you had to go see your uncle in the hospital. How it wouldn't be right that you, his favorite nephew— the one he always talked about giving his vending machine company to—didn't visit him on his death bed.

He'll think you got scratch coming. He'll let you slide.

The next time you can't pay up, tell him you're short cuz you had to go to Duluth again to talk to lawyers. Your uncle's making you executor of his estate, which means your grubs will control the loot.

He'll cut you more slack.

The trick is to string your bookie out like you're catching a carp. First your uncle gets better. Then he goes back at the hospital. Then he got a spleen miscarriage. Then he recovers.

To make it look good, carry a picture of Keith Richards in your wallet. Pretend it's your uncle. Your bookie ain't gonna know the difference. All he knows is the guy looks like he's gonna croak any minute, which means you'll have big scratch to make more stupid bets on Calgary and the Rams.

But sooner or later, your bookie will get to figuring there ain't no uncle. By this point, hopefully you're on a winning streak and paid off your debts.

Then again, there ain't a chance in hell of that.

Which leaves you three options:

1.) Tell your woman you heard they're hiring at a rendering plant in Arkansas. Get your ass down there right quick.

2.) Get beaten to death with a steering wheel lock.

3.) Rat your bookie out.

Option One ain't that good. First off, Arkansas is hot and all they ever eat is grits, which is basically Cream of Wheat, only they can't spell that so they call it grits.

Option Two is a little better, seeing as how if you bet on the Rams, you ain't never gonna amount to much anyways. Problem is, by the time you get reincarnated, you're gonna owe a &%$#load of child support.

That leaves Option Three: Rat the guy out. A course, Dr. Verne would never advise nobody to rat—except in special occasions, like saving your own ass.

If you can get a deal for probation, tell the feds all you know. The bookie goes away for ten years, you clear up your debts, and you can start thinking up new lies to tell your woman.

This is what financial guys call sound money management.

13

EARN JACK & SCORE CHICKS THROUGH THE LOST ART OF KIDNAPPING

Dear Dr. Verne:

I got this problem. They're trying to wussify me.

I had a good job fixin' lawn mowers at Sears. One day me and the boss got to fighting. That was the beginning of my problems.

I lost my job. Now I'm stuck working in some wussy-ass hotel.

I wanted to work at one of them classy places. The place I work for don't even got vibrating beds or PBR at the bar.

I just got word from my friend down in Missouri. He got a brand new bass boat, a huge house (it's a double-wide) and is about to get hitched with a girl that can tune his truck. How can I compete with this?

—Wussified in Rapid City

Dear Wussified:

Working at a hotel ain't gonna get you the good life of double-wides and bass boats. Problem is, you're stuck in Rapid City.

Last week I was reading how the fastest growing jobs there is retail sales and cashier. Women ain't partial to sparking with guys whose main duty is to say, "Would you like a non-smoking room with a view of the stock yards?" on account of you couldn't afford plastic covers for their good couch.

Which is why you gotta change careers. The way I'm thinking, you need one of them decent careers where the money's good, the hours is short, and most of your time's spent sleeping or doing beer bongs.

I'm talking kidnapping.

Used to be this was a decent trade for white trash. A guy could nab a couple of rich fruities, collect some decent ransom, then retire to one of them vacation paradises like Dubuque on the fruits of his labor.

I'm figuring a good person to kidnap would be a gas station attendant or a mailman. They both got good jobs that pay over minimum, which means you could probably hold 'em ransom for 135 bucks or more. Think about all the chicks you'll be scoring when you flash that 135 around the bar.

But since I'm doing all the thinking here, I should at least get a twenty percent cut. It wouldn't be right to ice out your ol' pal Verne, on account of my old lady can't tune a truck neither, and I'm falling behind on her electrolysis payments.

14

THE NORTHERN TRASH INDEX

Babies needed to discourage your in-laws from thinking you're a lesbian:

6

Legs you'll have left after passing out on train tracks:

0

Average times it takes to pass the drivers license test:

7

Dollars you'll get from a pawn shop for a stolen circular saw:

10

Extramarital affairs for the average Northern White Trash woman:

17

Extramarital affairs for the average Northern White Trash man:

62

Times you've spiked your husband's Old Style with Liquid Plumber because of that last statistic:

9

Average number of beers consumed at a felony pre-sentencing party:

326

Joints it takes to drive a forklift off a loading dock:

5

Number of beers it takes to bribe the plant
urinalysis tester:

100

Proper number of years to wait before repainting
your house:

58

Times you've taken a restraining order out against
your husband:

11

Average number of people wearing blaze orange hunting
jackets at a Northern Trash wedding:

24

Bags of beer nuts you'll get by trading in the antlers of a
10-point buck at a bar in the Upper Peninsula:

39

Average dollar value of the jewelry stolen from the cas-
ket at a Northern Trash funeral:

28

Average number of death threats needed to get your
damned HMO to cover your claim for a broken elbow you
got in a brawl at Shea Stadium:

4

Number of lies you told to the Job Service counselor during your weekly meeting:

16

Number of teeth in the average North White Trash Male
over age 27:

8

Shots fired during the average family picnic:
21
Times your uncle Mel's been arrested for
indecent exposure:
4
Blows it takes to kill your boss with a claw hammer:
3

15

THE TOKEN CHAPTER ABOUT
DEEP & CULTURAL STUFF

"What's wrong, Verne? You gone fruity?"

That's probably what you're thinking on account of I got this chapter about deep and cultural stuff.

See, most people don't think of us Northern White Trash as deep. They figure the most serious stuff we talk about is whether Pennzoil got a decent viscosity level or not.

The problem is trash start to getting them inferiority complexes whenever they get around deep stuff.

Say your woman is tired of you laying on the couch all weekend watching the Cubs-Montreal series. And say she gets one of them notions to haul your butt down to the art museum, so's you can have some deep quality time.

Of course you're gonna protest. "Sit your ass down," you say. "Ain't no better art than watching Blauser play a deep short on Astroturf."

Which, of course, ain't gonna work. She's gonna slap you harder than a truck stop waitress.

Which means you best get your butt moving, unless you wanna be eating White Castle for the next month.

Which means you're gonna be surrounded by pointy-heads with berets all afternoon, who's gonna stare like you're some kind of moron for wearing your Seahawks zubaz and the Loren's Mobile Home Retirement Community t-shirt your ma sent up from Tempe.

Don't worry. Faking like you're deep is easier than hijacking a truckload of laundry softener.

How To Be Held In Rapture

The first thing you notice is that everybody wears black at museums. It's like they're in mourning cuz their ma's all died at once.

This is the official uniform of Authentic Deep People.

Now Deep People ain't good for much. They can't fire-bomb a scab's house or clean a walleye. But they're awful good at standing around museums staring at stuff and not saying a word, as if they drank a fifth of Jack and is watching *Naughty Car Wash Babes II*.

But they ain't drunk. They're just held in rapture.

I don't exactly know what rapture is, but it's important to being deep. The trick is to stare at a painting or sculpture for a long time, pretending it's so meaningful you can't talk. Then, after about a half-hour, say something about its "gripping isolation" or its "transcendent insight into the systematic betrayal of faith," just so folks don't think you're a mute.

It don't matter that no one will know what the hell you're talking about. That's the point of being deep.

Faking Like You Know French

If there was truth in advertising, most paintings would be titled, "Globs of Paint Hastily Thrown on Canvas & Hocked at a Gallery Because I Had to Pay the Rent."

Problem is, Deep People figure this stuff got metaphors and symbolism in it. Which brings us to Lesson No. Two: Always pretend art has meaning, even if it looks like it was knocked out by a two-year-old who got a hold of some paint while her ma was on the phone.

Say you're at a museum with the old lady, and you is staring at an eighty-foot canvas with one red dot in the middle. Strike a deep and thoughtful pose, hand on chin, like you're captivated by its power. Then, after a long silence, say something French.

Of course, you don't know no French. Which is why you gotta use the names of hockey players. "I find a disturbing sense of *gaetan duschene* in her work."

The Beret People will be intimidated by your deepiocity. They won't notice the painting reminds you of a former winger for the Minnesota North Stars.

The Performance Art Scam

Before the 1960s, this was called Stuff People Do Before Becoming A Ward Of The State Mental Health System. Then someone figured out that Deep People would pay top dollar to see loonies.

So a bum, tired of sleeping on heating grates, laid down on the floor of the Chicago Museum of Art, stuffed himself in a giant Ziploc bag, and called his work, "This Is Just As Good A Place As Any To Sleep."

Performance art was born.

The bum became the toast of the White Wine & Brie Circuit. One problem: He suffocated to death. So some other bums cashed in when they left his body in the museum to rot, calling their project, "Works in Decomposing Carcass."

They are now tenured professors at Berkeley and get to sleep in their offices.

Sculpture's Red Green Period

There was a day when you could slap up an eight-footer of some naked Greek guy and everyone was happy. Problem was, everybody could understand it, which means no one could feel superior, which means it wasn't very good art.

In order to become deeper, sculptors started welding rusty gas grills and old lawn furniture together, calling it "Interdisciplinary Works In Stuff Welded Together That The Artist Couldn't Unload At His Garage Sale." They claimed it was a metaphor for the decline of Western Civilization.

The Red Green Period was born.

It ain't easy to fake your way through this stuff. But a few handy lines will help you pawn yourself off as one of them aficionados of sculpture.

Say you're trying to hit on a babe from the mail room. She's going to night school at the community college, taking up legal secretarying. You figure she's deep.

So you take her to the new exhibit of the noted New York sculptor to see his greatest work: a propane tank painted with white enamel. Okay, so's it's just a propane tank, for chrissakes. But being deep and all, you fake like you're held speechless.

After the Standard Moments of Silence, you say something like, "It's lines speak to a piercing violation of the human psyche."

Then, you add, "I've always admired his work with utility industry hardware."

If the Beret People nearby nod their approval, say something critical. (Lesson No. Three: You can't be deep if you're not bitching about something.) Compare his work to another hockey player.

"Of course," you sniff, "his work is not equal to Lucien LaFreniere's, who was the master of the propane genre."

LaFreniere had a short career with the New York Islanders in the mid-'80s. Nobody'll know what the hell you're talking about. Which means you're deeper than them.

"Yes," they will agree as they slink away, intimidated by your insight. "LaFreniere was the forerunner of the modern propanists."

Your babe will think you're artsy and cultural. She'll want you to spend the night at her place.

If There's No Unshaven Detectives, It Must Be Deep

You got two simple rules for faking a film knowledge. Rule No. 2: Always call them films, never movies.

Film means it was directed by some guy with a thin mustache from Europe who don't read boxscores.

Movie means it was directed by some guy who's originally from Nebraska, but dyed his hair blonde, moved to

Hollywood, and started saying stuff like, "Love ya, babe. Ciao."

Rule No. 2: If it got no action and has subtitles and the camera stays glued to some lady for 15 minutes while she stares out the window and looks like her best hunting dog died, it's deep.

But if it's got unshaven detectives who break department rules to work with big-boobed babes to hunt down international terrorists with crewcuts named Hans, it ain't deep.

Say you're a woman who just got a job in the claims department at Lucifer Insurance. And say you got a hankering for the boss. He ain't that good looking, but he's a boss, which means he probably got ice cream and a good liquor cabinet back at his place.

So you pull out the skimpy wardrobe you got from your sister, who didn't need it after she quit the strip joint when she had her sixth kid.

It works. He asks you for a date before lunch time.

But instead of taking you to a bar, like decent Northern Trash would do, he takes you to some damned film festival about the great directors of Greenland. So you gotta fake like you're deep. Otherwise, you ain't scoring none of that liquor and ice cream.

The key to faking a film knowledge is citing the great masters.

Example: Say you just got done spending four hours on some damned double-feature with subtitles. You don't even know what language they was talking. As you stroll from the theater, say something like, "Ah, touches of Fellini."

Your date don't call your bluff. He's an insurance guy, for chrissakes. He thinks Greenland's an amusement park in Vermont.

"However," you add, "the cinematic minimalism was preponderantly influenced by Bergman, wouldn't you agree?"

This is a lock to work, since everybody knows the masters is supposed to be deep, but nobody's ever seen their movies.

Your date will nod his head in approval. He will realize you're deeper than him. He will change the subject to his theories on term life policies.

And the next time you go out, he'll take you to a *Die Hard* sequel.

16

MY GIRLFRIENDS SAY I GOTTA SET BOUNDARIES WITH EARL

Dear Dr. Verne:

I got me my mobile home from my ex in the divorce decree. While I been divorced from Earl for five months, I been letting him sleep over. I'm between men right now, and while he's not what I call a one-woman man, we do got us a history and two kids together.

Anyhow, now that our Saturday nights have become regular and all, he feels the trailer is his again. He's been leaving his beater truck in the yard. It's without a engine and you got to ride it Indian style, seeing hows there ain't no floor board.

Well, Dr. Verne, my girlfriends say I gotta set boundaries. What the hell does that mean? I mean, he ain't asked me to tattoo his name on my hindquarters, like he asked me when we was hitched. I just feel maybe I should draw the line somewheres, but least I get some lovin' and Earl leaves his Wild Turkey bottles and Old Mil cans for me to cash in so I can get the wee ones beans and Tang.

—*Cherri,*
Burlington, Vermont

Dear Cherri:

Boundaries is one of them things the feminisms thought up. It's a fancy way of saying you gotta kick Earl's ass. Basically, them feminisms figured if they made a bunch of rules, men would be too stupid to follow 'em, which would make women the rulers by default.

Even if he's a stiff, it's good to have a man around for cutting grass, hauling old car batteries to the compost pile or just having someone to bitch at when you're crabby or out of liquor.

Problem is, you don't wanna get too cozy. Say you meet one of them guys who does oil changes at Tires Plus. The guy probably makes top dollar, like $7.50 an hour, plus bennies. And say you take him home some night. It ain't gonna be good for starting a healthy relationship if Earl's passed out naked on the living room floor.

If I was you, I'd get me them boundaries. Start by telling Earl he gotta sleep in the truck just in case you bring the Tires Plus guy home. Let him know he can only sleep in the house when you're horny and there ain't no other decent men around.

Second off, don't let him use the remote. Nothing makes a man feel more unwanted than not getting to touch the channel surfer.

Finally, tattoo somebody else's name on your hindquarters, like Mel or Tires Plus. It don't matter who it is. Earl will be able to tell by your butt that he's permanently outta the picture, and that he should go back to Wanda, the broad he dumped you for when you got divorced in the first place.

If none of this works, shoot him. Men get to understanding real good when they got some buckshot in 'em.

17

10 Tips for Women Who's Ascared of Getting Stuck With A Loser

When God created the world, He started out with woman, seeing as how she had more complex architecture and plumbing. Besides, He was dying for conversation cuz He hadn't invented TV yet.

Anyways, it took Him damn near all week—three days working on the brain alone.

Then, late on the 6th Day, the hardware stores was closed. Knowing that He wouldn't get overtime for working Sunday, God just slapped together man with the leftover scraps and headed for the bar.

Which is why men ain't too smart. He figured if He just made 'em strong enough to haul the garbage out, there might be a use for 'em.

That's why I got this 10-point checklist for latching a man. It's to help you decide the difference between a worthless man—one who ain't great, but good enough to have babies with—and a low-down, nasty, lying, cheating man, which are only good for affairs.

The selection ain't good, but think of it like rummaging through the clothes bins at Goodwill. At least you got volume on your side.

1. Is he a pervert?

All men is perverts. But there's a big difference between regular perverts and gentlemen perverts. Regular perverts take you to Hooters on your first date and spend the night telling stories about the biggest jugs they ever seen. Which ain't classy, especially if they only got enough money for chicken wings.

Gentlemen perverts is at least self-respecting enough to buy you a decent meal and some plastic jewelry before trying to get you in the sack.

If your old man A.) named his reproductive unit after a World War II cargo plane; B.) still subscribes to National Geographic for the naked Amazon women; C.) has a job in human resources; chances are he's a pervert. Don't let him near your kids.

2. Does he live with his ma?

If he still lives with his ma, he's used to getting picked up after, which means you won't have time for affairs with the guys from the Paint & Sealant Department.

The good part is he's a mama's boy who'll be easy to smack around when he squawks about your Hamburger Helper. The bad part is he'll be too sissified to teach your kids the valuable lessons of life, like how to sweet talk the game warden when you're four muskies over limit.

It's best to get a guy who's been on his own for a few years. That way, if you clean every Christmas and don't ash on the carpet, he'll think you're Martha Stewart.

3. Does he work at a convenience store?

Convenience stores is bad for two reasons. First off, he'll only make six bucks an hour, which means a day's work only buys a 30-pack of diapers and a twelve of Grain Belt.

Second off, convenience store clerks is always getting shot. What happens if you got a big night at the Legion Hall planned, the old man gets shot, and he ain't home to babysit on time?

4. Can he fake a decent back injury?

A lot of women is attracted to stupid guys cuz they'll believe it when you tell 'em stuff like, "If you don't run to the store and get me a pack of cigs, you can catch AIDS." But he can't be too stupid.

Say your old man's faking a back injury to score workers' comp. But say his buddy, who's a contractor, offers him a side job busting a concrete driveway, which just happens to be at the house of his case worker, Reginald Grabowski.

The first clue might have been the name "Reginald Grabowski" stenciled on the mailbox.

But your old man, figuring there's gotta be dozens of Reginald Grabowskis in Powell Butte, Oregon, keeps slugging away with the maul. Next thing you know, he loses the workers' comp.

Yet he ain't smart enough to do the logical thing: Smash his foot with the maul, so he can get another workers' comp scam going.

That's why you don't wanna make babies with stupid guys. When you're old, your kids won't know how to scam, either. Then there'll be no one to buy you Mr. Pibb and lotto tickets.

5. Is he a fat pig?

This can be good or bad, depending on how you look at it. Most women don't like being married to a fat pig cuz it's like sleeping with a walrus. If you was attracted to walruses, you'd probably marry a real one, on account of zoo animals don't pay no rent and people throw food at you.

The good part is, if your old man gets fat enough, you can use him for insulation when the heat gets shut off.

6. Is he dainty?

Does your old man spend more time talking about his hair dryer than his power tools? Does he put mousse in his caulking gun? Does he have problems saying who's the points leader in the Winston Cup standings?

If so, he's probably a lawyer, which means he's good at bilking old ladies' trust funds, but he'd end up being a love toy for the Aryan Nation when he goes to prison. The ladies at the beauty parlor won't respect a woman who's sharing her man with a 320 pound guy named Otis.

7. Does he got manners?

You can tell a real gentleman cuz he'll always say something nice about your butt, no matter how big it is.

Say he's laying on the couch watching baseball. "Woman," he says, "could you score me another brewski?" As you leave the room he adds, "Your butt's so cute I should list it on the renter's insurance as jewelry."

That's class.

But what if he only says, "Woman, grab me another brewski." Then, as you leave the room, all he does is cuss out Roberto Hernandez for giving up a two-out single. This here's an example of no class, which means you should probably set him up with your sister. Then you can gossip about the moron she married at holiday get-togethers.

8. Does he flirt with other women?

This could be a sign that he's hound dogging truck stop waitresses when he's supposed to be at a strip joint with his buddies. Then again, a lotta ladies don't mind their men having affairs cuz they'll do less pawing on them. If it keeps the creep outta the house, all the better. Just make sure his ass is around when it's time to shovel the sidewalk.

9. Does he eat sissy?

Say your old man wants to propose. He's offering to take you to dinner, someplace classy. Naturally, you pick KFC. All the way there he's talking about saturated fat and cholesterol. Dump him.

If he don't like KFC, chances are he jogs and has a matching tennis outfit he hides at his ma's house. If you marry him, he'll be too dainty to defend your honor when your uncle paws your butt during the dollar dance at the wedding.

10. Does he still brag about his glory days?

Nothing worse than having an old man who thinks he's an athlete. Whenever he gets drunk, he'll be giving you the frame-by-frame account of how he won the rec league bowling title when he was fourteen.

Worse yet, you'll have to haul your ass to softball games all summer, making excuses to the other wives about why your husband couldn't snare a grounder if it was a naked lady with a twelve pack.

18

10 Tips for Keeping Guys Outta Divorce Court
(At least till next month)

Love is what you call your many splendored thing. Problem is, the guy with the splendor stops showing once you get hitched. Which is why you gotta be careful when selecting your woman.

This ain't TV. Only morons figure they're gonna score a total babe who can fry up a bass and hold a decent conversation about the Steelers' secondary.

The way I figure it, shopping for women is like shopping for trucks. Sure, you want the extended cab with the brush guard, snow plow and the heavy duty suspension. But if you score half that, you're doing pretty good.

That's why I got this 10 point checklist. If your woman passes five or more, it's safe to pull the trigger.

This don't guarantee nothing. But according to the rules of Northern White Trash Etiquette, you got at least four divorces before people start looking at you weird.

1. Make sure she ain't a pig

You don't want no wife who cleans like a drunk maid from one of them rent-by-the-hour motels. That's why you gotta do research. Ask yourself these questions: Does she draw Christmas decorations in the grease on the kitchen wall? Does she leave cig butts in the shower drain? Is the crumbs on her carpet thick enough to clean with one of them leaf blowers?

If you're answering yes, you're gonna need a night job to pay for the maid.

2. Make sure she don't got a sister who's way better looking

Say you knock up your woman. Then, on your wedding night, you finally meet her sister from Kansas, who's way better looking than the one you're marrying. Next thing you know you'll be trying to score with her in the garage at family gatherings.

Romance ain't real pleasurable with a Lawn Boy stuck in your back. What's more, your woman's brothers'll get wind of it and beat you till you talk like a figure skater.

Ask to see the family pictures before you get to knocking her up.

3. Can she cook a decent steak?

Nothing worse than working hard all month to collect the unemployment check, then having your woman make a steak that looks like it got cooked by an arc welder.

It ain't a bad idea to road test her on the cooking before the wedding bells. Have her cook a steak after she just pounded a quart of Beam, or after you just got home with lipstick on your pants zipper and called her Lucy by mistake.

If she can still nail the steak under these normal conditions, you got yourself a keeper.

4. Can you whup her ex?

The first time your woman takes her ex to court for being behind on the child support, he's gonna show up at your place. What you gotta know is, can you kick his ass? And if you can't, is it worth shooting him, seeing as how dead guys don't usually pay support and you'll probably have to get a job?

5. Make sure she ain't no temperance woman

Say you and your buddies drop by the bar after work. And say one of 'em is celebrating because his daughter got out of prison. He wants to buy a round of shots. But you gotta pass, on account of your woman will squawk if you come home hammered for dinner.

Pretty soon all your buddies is gonna look at you like you got naked pictures of Barbara Bush hanging in your garage.

Never marry a woman who got less than two drunk driving arrests. If she's a lush herself, she may clean the liquor cupboard out, but at least you won't have to apologize when you park the truck in the living room.

6. Watch out for them woman's equalities

It's okay if ladies want equal pay. Then they can buy rounds too. But there's two things a guy's gotta have total control over: the channel surfer and the power tools.

If she don't understand this, she's probably from California. Unload her before you go fruity and start drinking wine that don't come in a box.

7. Is her hips sturdy enough for baby making?

The last thing you want is some skinny lady who whines like a college boy during labor. Chances are she's gonna cut you off at two kids. Which means the guys down at the plant'll be calling you a wuss cuz you don't have enough little shavers for a pit crew.

Me, I'd take her to the doc and get her hips measured. If they ain't baby making caliber, get yourself one of them prenuptial agreements that says if she don't give you at least five babies, you can trade her in for a real wife.

8. Will she pork out on you?

A lot of women start out skinny, have five or eight kids, then get to looking like a Coast Guard flotation device. If she thinks a two-pound bag of Doritos is a before-supper appetizer, you're looking at some serious oatmeal butt down the road.

The good part is she'll be too fat to get a job as a stripper or have affairs with your cousins. The bad part is that making love will be like wrestling a giant Polish sausage.

9. Does she got a union job?

Union jobs is better than winning the lottery, on account of you can't drink it all up in one night. If she's good at earning and saving, you can stay home and play Mr. Mom.

This ain't as wussified as it sounds. Just feed the kids donuts and let 'em play in the street. Meanwhile, you can spend your days at the hardware store or watching reruns of monster truck rallies on satellite.

10. Will she rat you out?

Last thing you want is a woman who ain't honest. If you get caught in bed with your aunt, she might get pissed and tell the cops about all them highway signs you stole for scrap aluminum.

So how do you tell if she's honest? Ask if she'd rather sleep with you or Billy Ray Cyrus. If she says you, dump her before she rats you out on that feed mill burglary you did last week.

19

CAN CHICKS EVER REALLY RESPECT AN ACCOUNTANT?

Dear Dr. Verne:

I am an accountant and I live in San Diego. I can't satisfy my wife in bed. Can you tell me how to please a woman?

—*Clueless in California*

Dear Fruity Accountant:

You being an accountant and all, you can't expect your woman to get excited about going to bed with 178 lbs. of blubber and gristle. But if you insist on trying, I got some surefire ways to please women, which might even work for accountants.

First off, you gotta set what you call your romantic ambiance. I'd start with some soothing love music, like ZZ Top or Sammy Hagar.

Then I'd make her one of them candlelight dinners. Bring out some nice appetizers, which is what fancy guys call the stuff you eat when you're too hungry to wait for supper. Nothing shows a woman you got class better than deep fried cheese sticks. But if you don't want to stink up the house with the deep fryer, just throw some Cheetos in a cereal bowl.

Now most fruity guys %$#& up by going next with a salad. When you make your woman a salad, you're basically saying to her: "I eat the same stuff as rabbits."

I'll clue ya, pal: Women don't get excited about sleeping with rabbits. They're looking for lions, which means you gotta go straight to the main course: pot pies.

Nothing says romance better than a Swanson's turkey pot pie. Turkey is a bird, which is kind of like a dove, which is the symbol of love. Make sure you point this out in case she don't get it.

Now she's melting outta your hands.

It's time, my friend, to repair to the bedroom—or the sofa if the bedroom got no TV. This is where a lotta white trash get stuck. Guys is always asking me, "Yo, Verne, what's the etiquette of watching TV when you're supposed to be satisfying the old lady?"

I judge this by the caliber of the game. Say it's a dainty West Coast game, like the Lakers-Golden State. For that I don't mind turning down the sound. But if it's something good, like Pistons-Cavs, no decent woman should expect to get your full attention. If your woman squawks about stuff like this, you're an asshole for marrying her and you deserve it.

Anyways, at this point you ain't gonna have no problems. The pot pies and ZZ Top already got her purring like them babes on the 1-900-NAUGHTY line. All you got to do is sit back, watch Grant Hill and let her do the work.

And when she asks about them miraculous sexual powers, don't forget to tell her you learned it all from Dr.
Verne.

You Don't Know Nothing About Chicks

Dear Dr. Verne:

I was very disappointed after reading your worthless
advice to Clueless in California on how to satisfy a woman
in bed. If ZZ Top, Cheetos and pot pies satisfy your white
trash woman, she must be faking it.

To please a woman, a real man needs to learn about a
woman's body, pay attention, take a lot of time and do
some of the play/work. You need lessons from a real
woman.

—*Bay Area Babe*

Dear Lady:

It sounds like you been going to too many of them
woman studies classes, otherwise you wouldn't be yam-
mering like this. As an expert in this field—seeing as how
I seen more backseats in bar parking lots than any man
alive—let me clue you on satisfying the ladies.

First off, decent white trash wouldn't be interested in
no woman who didn't like ZZ Top and pot pies. Right
thinking guys know if their woman is eating fruity &%$#
like salads and 58-grain pasta, they won't got big enough
hips to do some decent child-bearing.

Now about faking orgasms: Of course they are. How
many ladies you know is gonna have orgasms when
they're bedding down with some stinky guy who spent the
last 10 hours fixing mufflers? That's why white trash

ladies look at guys the same as food: volume is better than quality.

Take tonight, for your example here. All that's on cable is the Clippers-Vancouver, which is fruity West Coast ball, which means they're going dainty in the paint. Plus my dart league don't play tonight. Which means I got nothing else to do, which means me and the little missus is gonna bring the Power Ranger in for servicing about 17 times.

Now I ain't claiming all them's gonna be quality operations. But say I hit just .235, which is your basic backup shortstop batting average. That means I'm still knocking down four Big O's a night. You telling me your sensitive ponytail guy can hit with that kind of power?

Now about learning women's bodies: Hell, most white trash learn this by age four, when they're old enough to steal the old man's Hustler.

I hate to say this, lady, but I think you ain't being tolerant of our cultural diversity. I'm thinking you need that sensitivity training so's you can learn to accept differences in others.

20

SKIPPY, BRITTANY & WHY THE CELL PHONE PEOPLE AIN'T GOOD AT LOVE

A lot of Northern White Trash think it's good being a yuppie, seeing as how they get paid way more and don't have to drink vending machine coffee or date women who spit tobacco on the carpet.

Same goes for Northern White Trash ladies. They figure if they ditch the spandex and quit chewing their gum like some goddamned woodchuck, they could land one of them guys named Chad. The good thing about guys named Chad is they don't smell like roofing tar and got little stockbroker muscles so you can smack 'em around if they get outta line.

Problem is, yuppie life ain't all it's cracked to be. See, yuppies is like a baby varmint who lost his ma. They're out there all alone in the woods of life, dainty little guys who don't know how to hunt or shoplift. They're defenseless. Which is why they wear them cute sweaters tied around their neck, the international signal for "Can someone point me to the nearest Gap?"

But say you wanna date Chad. And say you gotta bring him home to the family on Thanksgiving for approval. Your uncles is gonna be in the living room watching football and swapping drywalling stories. They're gonna take one look at Chad, pet him on the head and make 'em fetch beers all afternoon.

And it ain't gonna look good when your ma sets him a place at the kids' table.

But say you don't believe me yet. Say you're still thinking about dating a yuppie. Let me clue you about your average yuppie date:

Skippy Finds The One

Skippy's talking wine with the waiter, trying to be impressive, like he's got a thin mustache and a ascot or something. The waiter ain't buying, but he ain't letting on either. Each table is worth twenty bucks in tips. Thirty if he kisses ass hard enough. That'll pay a month's worth of cable. And if Skippy's willing to spring for the cable, the waiter's willing to not smack him while Skippy talks outta his ass about wine.

Skippy's looking good tonight. He got the 90210 sideburns and so much hair spray it's damn near bulletproof. There ain't no mustard stains on his navy blue blazer. It don't smell like smoke or beer either. You can tell he never wore it to a wedding.

Most guys wouldn't have the balls to wear that tie, all bright yellow and orange and green. But Skippy's going somewhere in this world. The bright colors is his way of saying, "Hey, I got bad taste in ties."

Brittany's his biggest score since Christy Gordter back at Georgetown. Skippy was gonna be a lawyer. Christy was gonna be a trophy wife. She never put out. He still got a complex.

Which is why he flunked the lawyer exam five times. Which is why he's now selling real estate.

These days he's gone to signing his name Emerson "Skippy" Thorwell E.W.A., the initials being real estate speak for "I slept through this two-hour seminar and now I got impressive initials after my name." He got a red LeBaron convertible. Cranks the public radio, figuring chicks will think he's deep.

Brittany wears enough makeup that most folks think she oughtta get a hazardous waste permit from the EPA. She went to Princeton, majored in English. That's why she's working downtown at a law firm.

They're sitting at the overpriced restaurant, the kind with the cloth napkins and so many goddamned forks you figure the manager's taking kickbacks from a silverware salesman.

Skippy's making small talk about how busy it is at the office. How he's gonna close on twenty-three—or was that three?—houses this month. How his clients is always trying to hire him, seeing how professional he is. How he thinks the boss is looking to promote him, let him run his own office. Maybe even get more initials after his name.

Brittany don't make eye contact. Once in a while she nods, throws a smile his way. But mostly she's scoping the room.

She dates three, four, five nights a week. She already slept with all the single guys at the law firm—half the married ones, too. All Brittany wants is to settle down, have some babies and shop. But now she's 29. If push come to shove, she'd be willing to skip the first two and just shop.

She ain't impressed by the flowers Skippy got her. Carnations, $9.99 a dozen on sale. She knows the prices of 'em all. And she wasn't impressed by no public radio music either. Her head gets to hurting every time she hears them goddamned violins.

Skippy orders the $29 dinner with the name you can't pronounce. Brittany orders the $43 steak. Why be stupid about it? she figures. He's picking up the tab.

Skippy does the talking over dinner. He tells her how he pumped in 28 points in a pickup basketball game at the Y the other night. How his dad made it rich in the welcome mat business. How the old man wants him to take over the company, seeing as how smart Skippy is.

But he don't want no handouts—except for the red LeBaron and the monthly allowance and the free condo, which don't really count.

Later they go dancing at one of them clubs where the music's so loud you scream at each other like deaf guys. Skippy yells into her ear about how he's thinking on settling down. Just as soon as he gets the big promotion with more money and initials. Probably buy one of them big houses in them golf course subdivisions with the grass that never gets no weeds.

Brittany smiles, one of them smiles that look like they're held up by reinforced steel cable, and goes back to scoping the room. Skippy goes to the can.

A guy named Ted slides up to the bar. He tells Brittany about how he's gonna make partner at the accounting firm he works at. Just as soon as he gets promoted outta the mailroom. She gives him her number.

It's two in the morning. Skippy walks Brittany to her apartment door, then stands there, doing his best impression of a basset who wants out of the rain. She feels obliged to ask him in, seeing as how that steak was 43 bucks and all.

Skippy makes his move. Brittany don't resist. Might as well, she figures. None of them lawyers call much anymore.

Skippy pumps away on top of her. She thinks of Ted. Could he really go from the mailroom to partner? He must be good at delivering mail. What kind of salaries do partners get? She figures it's gotta be somewhere around the six digits, which's enough to crank some serious firepower into her Marshall Fields card.

She starts shopping in her mind for new blouses, new wallpaper for the kitchen in that gated golf course subdivision that they damn well better get to buying before Skippy snatches it up.

She hears Skippy groan. She starts to squeal, trying to fake an orgasm, but ends up sounding more like one of them squishy bathtub toys. Skippy don't notice. He's pounding away, her squealing making him feel like Antonio Banderas, or maybe a guy who just got outta prison.

He finally rolls to the side of the bed, trying to catch his breath. Brittany asks him to leave; she's gotta work in the morning. She takes a shower. Skippy lets hisself out.

Brittany meets Ted for lunch the next day. They do the bone dance in the Chili King bathroom.

By 10 a.m., Skippy's told his ma he's found The One. He'll be bringing her out for Sunday dinner. You're gonna love her, ma.

He does imitations of Brittany's squeal for the guys at the office. They ain't impressed. It sounds like one of them squishy bathtub toys, they tell him. Skippy don't care. He calls Brittany all afternoon, leaving love poems on her answering machine.

Brittany got 16 messages when she gets home. She listens to the first few, then erases 'em. The phone keeps ringing. She lets the machine get it. She's busy, watching Harry Hamlin on the made-for-TV movie.

She wonders if Harry's married, how much he gets paid, if he ever dates office managers, or just big stars like Meredith Baxter.

She pulls her knees up to her chest, resting her chin on her sweat pants. She dreams of wallpaper in the gated golf course subdivision where she and Harry's gonna live.

21

RONNY'S NORTHERN TRASH GUIDE TO COURTING PROPER

In Chapter 20, we learned if you're gonna be a yuppie, chances are you gotta eat food with names you can't pronounce, and your woman's gonna be boning guys named Ted in the Chili King bathroom.

In Chapter 21, we learn how decent, right thinking Northern Trash oughtta be courting:

Ronny's Got A Woman

Ronny's mauling his face with a napkin, trying to get the thousand island outta his beard. Eating proper ain't his specialty.

See, Ronny's a big man, going somewheres around 6-3, 270. From a distance, he looks like that Abominable Snowman, or maybe just a guy who's got too much liking for pork chops. His is the kinda hands made for pulling engine blocks and laying sheet rock, not for trying to stuff no bird food in his mouth.

Siss don't seem to mind. It's her first night out in three months.

They're sitting at the Bonanza, wolfing hard on the all-you-can-eat salad bar. Ronny been telling her it's the best in town, on account of it got pickled herring and them Swedish meatballs that look better than the naked ladies over at B.J.'s Lounge.

Hell, it's kinda romantic too. From where they're sitting, they got a good view of the Radisson, which so happens to be the fanciest hotel in St. Paul. Ronny knows on account of his boss got married there. Had an open bar. He barfed on damn near every inch of that hotel.

Which is why most right thinking Northern White Trash knows better than to have a open bar.

Ronny, he been married before. Two times. The first one was Linda. She was his high school sweetheart, a dispatcher for Yellow Cab with one of the biggest damn butts you'd ever seen. Her friends called her Little Canada Butt, on account of she was from Little Canada and had that big butt. Linda, she didn't care. "At least it's paid for," she'd say.

They got married in September. He was 19. Linda was 18. They got separated by October. Divorced before Christmas. Ronny says it's because he came home sick one day and found The Butt in bed with a cab driver from Pakistan, or maybe Norway. He couldn't tell which on account of all the blood.

Carla, Ronny's second wife, they was married four years, till she fell asleep in her rig and drove it through a Perkins somewheres in Indiana.

Ronny been thinking about Siss for months. If you was asking him, Siss was the babe to end all babes. But he was ascared to pull the trigger.

Was about six months ago that she dumped her old man. Got herself a job doing invoices at Able's Construction, trying to keep away from the creep. Ronny, he noticed her right away. She had auburn hair that wasn't fake, curled at the ends everyday, even when it was raining.

Sure, guys might say she was a bit on the heavy side. But what the hell, Ronny figured. The woman had three kids. If she didn't get to porking out a bit after that, she'd have to be one of them anorexics.

Besides, Siss was the only lady in the office who didn't use the F-word. Always smiled when he dropped by to get his checks. Made a damn fine cup of coffee.

But Ronny never talked to her till the day Phil, her ex, came to the office. Seems Phil was the kind who liked to beat on women, which is why Siss dumped him. But Phil was also on the stupid side. He started yelling about Siss being a bitch right there in the Able office.

Rule No. 1 about cussing your ex-wife: Do it at an insurance agency. Do it at a department store. Do it anywheres they got sissy guys in ties working. But don't go cussing no lady at a construction company.

Ronny was the first to grab Phil. Before you knew, there were six or seven guys on him. They took him outside.

The guys, they still talk about the beating they gave Phil. He looked like the Elephant Man after open face surgery, all puffy and mangled. These days, he makes sure to pay the child support on time.

Siss appreciated the gesture. Brought Ronny one of them Hostess pies for breakfast the next day to show her thanks. Ronny asked her to dinner. Bonanza. Best eating in town.

Siss makes a third trip to the salad bar. She wolfs down the chicken fried steak like a guy who just dug 100 yards of post holes. Ronny smiles. Few things is prettier than a woman with a good appetite.

Ronny's telling her how they been sheet rocking this job over in Highland Park, where a rich man's rehabbing this old railroad mansion. You should see the place, he's telling her. Oak archways. A kitchen practically the size of New Mexico. And a porch that—once they get the rot out and sand down the railings—would be perfect for sipping a little Jim Beam and watching the summertime rain.

Ronny tells her how his goal in life is to buy a place like that. Figures he could pick one up off 7th Street, in the shade of the old Schmidt plant, for less than fifty grand. Sure, she'll need some work. Maybe take a year or more before it's presentable.

Be nice to settle down in a place like that with a good woman, he tells her, checking to see if she gets the hint. But Siss ain't paying much attention. Damn, that's some good chicken fried steak.

After dinner, Ronny invites her out to Lou's Viaduct Inn. It's a classy place, he tells her. Got computer darts and 50-cent pool and drinks for a buck-fifty. Damn if that bartender Jerry don't make the best fuzzy navel in town. The ladies sure go for that.

But Siss says she gotta go. Things is still tight at home. Got to get rid of the babysitter before the bill gets too high. Besides, she's probably got her clothes half off with her boyfriend right now.

Ronny says he understands, tries to smile, but he knows he's getting the high hat. He wonders what he did wrong. Was it the cole slaw that kept getting in his beard? The time he accidentally cut the cheese while they was waiting at the biscuit tray?

He knows the guys at the bar'll ride him hard if he comes back alone. Hell, it's only eight o'clock. They drive home without talking.

At the door, Ronny's tells her how much he enjoyed hisself. How it was a pleasure to have the company of such a fine lady. He asks if she wouldn't mind him paying the babysitter, seeing as how times was tight.

Siss pecks him on the cheek. Asks if he wouldn't mind coming in. Her sister borrowed her a couple of Chuck Norris videos to watch. Did Ronny like Chuck Norris?

Ronny follows her in, even though he thinks Chuck Norris is a fruity. The guy's always wearing turtlenecks, for chrissakes. Now he's got a TV show about Texas Rangers. Pussy. If he was a real cop, he'd be working in a place that got better crime, like Detroit or Pittsburgh or Minneapolis, not busting some cattle rustlers who's dressed up like tour guides from Rapid City.

But Ronny ain't letting on. "Yeah, I love that guy," he tells her.

The kids is all in their pajamas, running around the living room like drunk Teamsters at the end of a strike. The babysitter's on the phone, fighting with her boyfriend, who just so happens to be her cousin too.

It's a nice looking place, Ronny thinks to hisself. Decent panel job, whoever did it. Good couch too. Still got the plastic on so it don't get no baby drool. Siss got her wedding pictures on the wall, only Phil's been crossed out with a marker.

Siss sends the babysitter home, puts the two littlest to bed. Her oldest girl sits between 'em on the couch as Chuck pretends he's a Chicago cop on TV. He's wearing that goddamned turtleneck again. Chuck would get his ass kicked if he ever showed up at Lou's, Ronny thinks to hisself.

Siss' oldest is a good kid. She got big ears and her teeth kinda look like the mangled grill of an old Dodge, but she's cute in her own way. Ronny wouldn't mind calling her his own, on account of he never had none for hisself. The Butt was too busy boning cab drivers from Pakistan or Norway to get to reproducing. Carla always said she'd have some, but that ended when she left her Mack in the no smoking section of that Indiana Perkins.

One of the little ones is crying in the bedroom. Siss goes to lay with him, says she'll be right back. Hour later, she still ain't there. Ronny puts in another Chuck and lets the oldest lay on his lap.

The next morning, Siss finds him sleeping on the couch. The TV's still running, and Ronny's snoring louder than the grinder at the packing plant she used to work at. Her oldest is snuggled under one of his arms.

She makes him bacon and eggs. He shovels her driveway and rehangs her gutters on account of the roof is rotting.

Siss' sister comes over late in the morning. Siss blabs to her like a school girl about the nice man she found. How much her kids like him. How he made Phil look like the Elephant Man. How he's outside right now fixing the gutters, which she'd been on Phil about for more than a year. That prick.

There's still decent men out there, Siss says. You just gotta look.

Ronny comes in to let Siss know the gutters is done. He sees her blabbing, figures it's time to go. Got some work to do, he says.

But Ronny don't feel like working. It's Sunday afternoon. The Vikings is on. He heads over to Lou's where the guys'll be.

Ronny orders up a Schmidt. The guys want to know how it went. Did he get any? Was her boobs really as big as they looked?

Ronny tells 'em to shut up. Tells 'em that gentlemens don't talk about a lady like that, and if you creeps was gentlemens you'd know that. But he can't be pissed at 'em. He can't be pissed at the Vikings either, who's down by 10 again to Detroit. Goddamned Barry Sanders.

He sits at the bar, staring at the big screen. All he can think about is a place off 7th Street, Siss' kids playing in the house, and him sitting on the porch, sipping on some Jim Beam and watching that summertime rain.

22

How to Score with Bob & Impress Human Services

Dear Dr. Verne:

I found me a real good man. His name is Bob. He was working on the construction site near my office. One day I was outside for my smoke break and he was sitting down on one of his union-negotiated breaks and we got to talking.

Then his union went on strike, so we spent about a week doing the bone dance in my trailer. It was all romantic and stuff, but then they settled the strike. Human Services brought back my kids about the same time.

Since then, we haven't been able to get no quality time with Bob. I ain't opposed to locking the young ones outside on a nice day for a couple of seconds, but with this damn rain, they keep tracking mud on my green shag carpet and I have to wipe down my plastic furniture covers. Any suggestions?

—Searchin' for Solitude in Massachusetts

Dear Searchin':

You got what them pointy heads call your parental dilemma. You can't be locking the kids out too long, on account of the neighbors will rat you to Human Services, who'll send your kids to live with them yuppies, who'll teach 'em not to shoot their 12-gauge at rats in the house, which means they'll be wrecked by the time you get 'em back.

Then again, a fine lady like you deserves to get her bone dancing in with Bob.

What you need is a tool shed.

Whenever I have Velvet or Sherry or Honey Bee over while the old lady's working the graveyard shift, I send the kids to the tool shed. I give 'em a bag of Marshmallow Mateys and tell 'em there's five bucks in it if they can shut up and pretend they're playing in a crackhouse with no electricity.

Seeing as how five bucks can buy a lot of candy cigs or a pawn-shop buck knife, the kids is happy to obey. That way they stay dry, so's they ain't dragging no mud in the house, and I got plenty of time to play jackhammer with them aforementioned ladies.

But say you ain't got a tool shed. Me, I'd think about locking 'em in one the Trans Ams you got on blocks in the yard. Tell 'em it's a space ship, and if they get out before you come back, their eyes'll get burnt up and they won't be able to play Atari no more. That'll teach 'em.

And if your old man happened to take the Trans Ams with him when he left, which ain't likely, Bob can make himself useful and dig a dry hole under the trailer. Tell the kids to play army and pretend it's a foxhole. Then toss a few firecrackers out the window from time to time to make it seem authentic.

This is what pointy-heads call nurturing their creativity. Human Services will be impressed.

23

Answers to the Most Commonly Asked Questions about Getting Hitched Proper

Is eloping bad financial management?

Dear Dr. Verne:

I'm engaged to Rocco, but I haven't told my daddy yet. He thinks Rocco's a lazy ass and says if he ever catches me and Rocco together, he'll cut out his throat with a chainsaw.

I tell him Rocco just got his GED and his old man's getting him on at the sanitation department, but daddy won't listen. I want to elope, but Rocco says that's bad financial management, on account of we'll miss out on all them presents. What should I do?

—Shonda in Trenton

Dear Shonda:

This Rocco's a keeper. He's got smarts enough to realize no matter how big of a scumbag he is, the rules of weddings say you gotta give presents. And seeing how Rocco's old man got a decent union job, you guys'll probably be into the serious presents, like power augers and season tickets to the Eagles. The way I figure it, even if your old man does slice up Rocco, you still get to score the free gifts and maybe now you could marry that A&P clerk you been sleeping with.

A question of class: charcoal gray or powder blue?

Dear Dr. Verne:

I'm marrying a handsome young man from Eugene. I know you won't approve, seeing as how he's from a dainty college town, but I love him just the same.

Anyways, I been fighting with his mom about the wedding. She wants the groomsmen to wear charcoal gray. I want them to wear powder blue. But since she's paying for the wedding, she wants it her way. Bitch. I don't think that's right.

—Tammy in Seattle

Dear Tammy:

Everyone knows powder blue is superior cuz it got class and hides the barf stains better. But that's what you get for consorting with a lesser class of people.

What you gotta do is express your feelings. Let her know this is your wedding, and that it's important to show class with some powder blue. If that don't work, when no one's looking, dunk her head in the bathtub until she sees it your way. This is what feminisms call being assertive.

What's the seating arrangements for inbred weddings?

Dear Dr. Verne:

I'm gonna marry my cousin Billy in August. Problem is, we don't know which side of the aisle to seat the guests, seeing how both of us is related.

—Mary in Fort Kent, Maine

Dear Mary:

Basic science tells me that none of your relatives is gonna have a clue, seeing as how they're inbreds. I'd worry more about getting 'em to use the chairs instead of laying on the floor. Arm your ushers with some cattle prods just to be on the safe side.

How's a guy to stop his relatives from stealing the silverware?

Dear Dr. Verne:

I got it made. I'm getting married to Sandy Bluderhousen. Her face ain't that good, but she's got a nice body and her old man runs the biggest construction company in Wyoming.

Here's my problem: Sandy's old man is springing for a reception at the Super 8. But I'm worried my relatives is gonna steal the silverware. I don't want Sandy's old man pissed at me, otherwise he won't give me one of them no-show jobs.

—Louie in Casper

Dear Louie:

One of the hottest things in weddings this year is metal detectors. That not only keeps your relatives from stealing the silverware, it also keeps 'em from bringing guns, knives and bats to the reception. That makes for fairer fights.

The last thing you need is one of your brothers getting liquored up and stabbing your father-in-law when he turns him down for a job. According to wedding experts, whacking in-laws ain't a healthy way to start a marriage. With metal detectors, you not only save on having to reimburse the hotel for all the stuff that gets stoled, but all the knife fights will be in the lobby, where they ain't your problem.

Who's my daddy?

Dear Dr. Verne:

I'm getting married, but my ma don't know exactly who my daddy is. The way she figures it, it could be one of about twenty guys who used to hang out at Myron's Tavern in Rockford in 1977. Which one should I ask to give me away?

—Monica in Kankakee

Dear Monica:

I'd use what you call your deductive reasoning here. You figure half of 'em gotta be dead or in prison, which knocks it down to ten.

Then I'd knock me out the two ugliest ones, on account if they're your father, you don't wanna know.

Then I'd kick out the four that don't got no money, on account of what's the use of getting a dad if he ain't gonna give you nothing for your troubles?

Now you're down to four. I'd tell 'em there's an open bar and invite 'em all. The one who's smart enough to drive all the way from Rockford gotta be your dad, on account of the other three's too stupid to get down your ma's pants if they ain't smart enough to go where the free liquor is at.

How to hide the fact that you're knocked up

Dear Dr. Verne:

I be getting married in February, but I'm already in the motherly way, if you know what I mean. What wedding gown would you recommend for hiding pregnancies?

—Lucy in Black River Falls, WI

Dear Lucy:

Seems you got two choices here. The first is to wear a normal wedding dress, on account of most people will just think you got a beer belly. That'll tell your husband's kin you're decent, down-home people, and you like a beer and a steak just as much as the next guy.

But if you wanna play this sneaky—which I don't know why you would, cuz most Northern White Trash women got a litter before they're married—I'd think about going casual. Wear something with class, like your Arctic Cat jacket or a Packers jersey. This sends a message to the audience that you got a pioneering sense of fashion, and that you ain't some moron who's gonna blow 40 bucks on a fancy wedding dress when it could pay for the first night of your honeymoon at the Red Roof.

How am I gonna get rid of all them blenders?

Dear Dr. Verne:

I'm worried about getting hitched. First off, how's a guy supposed to be married when there's so many barmaids I ain't nailed yet?

Second off, I figure I'm gonna end up with 17 blenders and no place to hock 'em. What you gotta say about that?

—*Harry, underneath the 9th Street Bridge*

Dear Harry:

Don't worry about the first part. It used to be called cheating on your wife, but then yuppies didn't like that name, so they changed it to open marriage. Just let your woman know that chicks dig you, that you gotta provide what you call your community service, and if she squawks she's just being selfish and setting a bad example for the young ones.

Besides, if you call it community service, the next time you get nailed on a burglary rap, you can bed down barmaids as part of your sentence.

Now about them blenders. You're right. There ain't what you call your good secondary market for small kitchen appliances. That's why when you send out the invitations, ask for handguns, power tools and TVs. These is what sells best at pawn shops and bars.

Can I still wear white if I'm a tramp?

Dear Dr. Verne:

I ain't exactly a virgin, and the priest knows, on the count of he's one of the guys who got to my flower. Can I still wear white? Or do I gotta go with my second choice, which is lime green?

—*Melva in Muncie*

Dear Melva:

Going on color alone, I'd be thinking about your lime green anyways. Personally, I always liked limes myself, cuz they go good with gin and you can rub 'em under your arms when you ain't had time to bathe.

But if you're truly wedded to the white, I wouldn't go worrying. (How do you like that pun, "wedded to the white"? That's what you call your deep literary maneuver. It took me an hour to think that up, so appreciate it.)

Anyways, the way I hear it, half the guys north of the Kentucky line done picked your flower, Melva. So if you was going by the virginity rules, you'd have to wear a funeral dress.

But the bright side is this: You ain't a looker. That means if anybody in the crowd got to pollinating you, he sure ain't fessing up to it.

Besides, what's the priest gonna say? According to the rules, priests is only supposed to sleep with altar boys. If he talks up about you, the guy's liable to get demoted to the Baptists, where they don't allow drinking and they're too cheap to even have a pope.

Which is better wedding music: Mariah Carey or Molly Hatchet?

Dear Dr. Verne:

My woman's been planning out our wedding like we's some candy-ass rich people. Most of it I don't mind, just so she leaves me outta it. But now she tells me she wants to have Mariah &%$#@#$ Carey music when we walk down the aisle. That's where I gotta draw the line.

See, a lotta guys from the plant'll be there, and I don't wanna have 'em see me walking to no fruity music, on account of they'll think I'm gay, which means I'll probably get transferred to management.

I was thinking about a compromise, like that Molly Hatchet, who's nice and lovey and all, but still rocks. But she says that's more like confirmation party music, and that if she can't have Mariah Carey, then she wants Whitney &%$#&% Houston. Are you kidding me? You gotta settle this, Verne.

—*Mike in Sioux City*

Dear Mike:

I'd say both of you're wrong. Weddings is basically boring as hell until you get to the drinking part. After my third marriage, I finally figured this out and got the church hooked up with big screen. That way, while you're doing the exchanging of vows, the crowd can watch Michigan-Ohio State so they don't start booing if it takes too long.

24

IS IT OKAY TO SHOOT MY NEIGHBOR?

Dear Dr. Verne:

I got a problem. It seems that my neighbor in the blue trailer (you know, the one with no roof) has been parking his Pinto in my driveway. This makes me mad cause I just done laid new gravel and I ain't got to use it yet.

I asked the preacher what I should do about it, and he said I should share (mostly cause I don't have a car anyway), but I don't wanna share.

What I want to know is this: Can I shoot him or should I put a certain yellow bodily fluid in his still?

By the way, can you get sick by drinking varnish?

—*Arnie in Sioux City*

Dear Arnie:

Your first mistake was talking to that preacher, who wasn't even good enough to get into the Priests' Union, so he had to become a preacher, who don't even say Mass, just some cheap-ass services.

But the preacher's right about one thing: A guy should share. It's okay to share stuff like pry bars or Pall Malls or the leftover ham your woman cooked in April, seeing as how it's green now anyways.

117

But driveways is a different story. It says so right in the Northern White Trash Constitution: "Thou shalt not covet thy neighbor's wife or driveway." Which means the guy in the blue trailer's probably a Satan worshipper.

In most states it's okay to shoot Satan worshippers, just so's you wait till hunting season and don't bag over your limit. But I don't figure the point of putting yellow bodily fluid in his still.

First off, it's against the Sacred Northern White Trash Ways to wreck a batch of liquor. Think about all the starving children in Africa who couldda drank it.

Second off, if you got yellow bodily fluids seeping outta you, I'd get your ass to a doctor. It sounds like your radiator might be leaking, and if your heart don't get enough coolant, it'll probably blow up and get guts all over your good recliner.

Now about the varnish. It says on the label you ain't supposed to drink it, but that's just sissy talk made up by pointy-head scientists who can't hold their liquor or their industrial wood treatments.

I say it's okay to drink, but it's better when you mix it with some OJ and gin.

25

TIPS ON WHAT SPORTS IS GOOD & WHAT SPORTS IS FOR GUYS NAMED CHAUNCEY

Sports is the religion of the Northern White Trash. Only it's better cuz they got it on big screen at bars and they don't mooch for money without giving you a beer.

But some people—mainly them TV fruities with the five-quart mousse jobs—get to defiling the name of the Cleanup Hitter In The Sky by saying them dainty games is sports.

Those of you with some Catechism probably recognize this from Corinthians: "And on the Seventh Day, God figured he was already in deep &%$# for violating the union rules. So he declared it a day of rest to keep OSHA off his ass.

"'Kick back,' he told all the guys in the shop. 'Have yourself a couple of brewskies, just so long as it ain't none of them designer beers from Europe. And for chrissakes don't be watching no fruity sports. You start watching tennis and the next thing you know everybody wants to work in human resources and we got nobody to run the jack-hammers.'"

But like a lot of things, people got to thinking the word of God was optional. Now it threatens what you call your very existence of the once proud Northern White Trash Nation.

Here's a handy guide to keep you in the good graces of God. Games is rated on a 1-10 Manliness Scale.

Auto Racing: 6

Racing's got engines and noise, which is manly. But they also got names of dish washing soap on their cars. Besides, sitting on your ass all afternoon ain't a sport. That's called being a parking ramp attendant.

Baseball: 8

The most drunk-friendly game. Since nothing ever happens, you can get hammered, fall out of the bleachers, crack your melon open, go to the emergency room, get 23 stitches, bar-hop your way back to the stadium and not miss a batter.

Basketball: 7

At this point you're probably saying, "What gives, Verne? Dennis Rodman got a red hairdo and wears dresses. And basketball got cute little matching outfits, just like tennis."

You got yourself a point here. Basketball's got too many skinny guys, like they might be vegetarians or against hunting. And them baggy shorts? Hell, why don't they just make 'em plaid and call it fratball? The first guy to drink two beers, get punched out and throw up on a sorority chick wins.

But at least basketball also got a lotta manly talk in it. You never hear no tennis announcer say, "Steffi Graf thunders into the paint and RIPS DOWN THE TOMAHAWK JAM OVER MARTINA HINGIS!"

Boxing: 3

Boxing used to be a sport. But then they got to charging for it on pay-per-view. God got pissed.

Corinthians 12:02: "And then God found out if he wanted to catch the Holyfield-Tyson fight, he was gonna have to spring 59 bucks on pay-per-view. God announced a boycott.

"'Next guy around here who orders pay-per-view gets his ass personally kicked by God,' He said. Though Paul figured he could whup God—seeing as how God wasn't exactly buff, on account of He spent most of his time laying on the couch bossing people around—none of the Disciples wanted to risk their cushy patronage jobs. And so it was decreed."

Figure Skating: 1

Guys named Boris prancing around in ballerina costumes to public radio music. There's no checking. No penalties. You never see 'em drop the gloves and duke it out with them other fruities in ballerina costumes. And I'll be damn sure you never heard nobody at the bar say, "I'll lay $50 and take the 6 points on the wuss in the pink outfit."

Football: 10

Fat guys smashing into each other in space uniforms. Almost as good as a Bruce Willis movie. All that's missing is the T&A and explosions.

Golf: -3

Here you got a bunch of guys named Lance and Chauncey. They're wearing cute little matching pastel outfits and riding around in go-carts. They ain't even cool go-carts, with duel exhausts or nothing. They're them plastic ones old men use for fetching groceries in Arizona.

Hockey: 11

The official sport of the Northern White Trash. Nothing better than toothless guys trying to filet each other with unsharpened lumber. The only problem is you can't pronounce their names, on account of half of 'em got drunk and spent their vowels on hookers and tattoos.

Olympics: 1

Gymnastics? Midget 14-year-olds boinging around on a mattress.

Skiing? Get a snowmobile, pal.

Diving? I could show you 20 guys in powder blue tuxes jumping into a Holiday Inn pool at a wedding reception. But they don't put it on ESPN and call it a sport. It's called 20 drunks falling in the water.

Bicycling? If your car got repossessed and you're stuck riding a bike, be a man, get a job or rob a 7-Eleven and earn for yourself. But don't think because you're broke you can call it a sport. If that was true, sitting on the steps drinking 40-ounce Millers at 11 a.m. on a Wednesday would be a sport, too.

Soccer: 1

You ever heard of England? It used to be this big country that captured all these extra countries all over the world. Then the English started playing soccer. Pretty soon they got so dainty they was getting their ass kicked by India, which got an army about as good as Utah's.

Tennis: 1

It beats the hell outta me why people wanna see them little foreigners hit a fuzzy ball. You can almost hear their ma's yelling, "Don't get your clothes dirty before the regatta, Skippy."

They even got a fruity way of keeping score. 6-love. Sounds like a sex line. "Call 1-900-6-Love and talk to Skippy, Biff and Douglas, three naughty little probate attorneys waiting to fulfill your hottest dreams."

26

WHERE ELSE CAN YOU GET PAID TO BRAWL & NOBODY CALLS YOUR PAROLE OFFICER?

Dear Dr. Verne:

I been reading your advice for some time now. Most times I agree with you, but you keep talking about hockey being a manly sport.

I got news for you, Verne, the only people who's good at hockey is pussy foreigners like French Canadians, Norwegians and Minnesotans. In case you don't know, French Canadians got their ass kicked outta Louisiana where even the deers is midgets, which means when you stuff 'em and hang 'em above the TV, people think you got a big clump of dog fur glued to the wall.

The only manly thing to come from Minnesota is the women. And if anybodies with names like Ole, Udder, Sven or Idder shows up at the trailer park, they gets beat up outta what we call principle.

So unless you're from French Canada or something, I suggest you stop calling someone on ice skates who talks

like he got beer foam coming outta his nose a manly type,
cause he ain't.

—*Buford in Des Moines*

Dear Buford:

I can tell you're worldly, seeing as how you got knowledge on foreign places like French Canadia. But you got it wrong about hockey.

Them French Canadias is at least part fruity, on account of they got French before their name. But for your info, Canadia is the Mecca of the Northern White Trash. Hell, Buford, wouldn't you wanna live where the government pays you to eat donuts, shoot caribou and pass out on the highway? It's true! I heard it on TV.

Now a lotta guys think Canadia is sissified on account of you don't hear about them getting in any decent wars. But my cousin Elmer, he lives in Winnipeg, and he says it's candy-ass to shoot somebody with a tank. Real men, they strap on the skates, grab some sticks, and see who can gut the other guy like a 12-point buck, man-to-man.

I ain't agreeing with you on Minnesota either. You're right they got some manly women up there, especially the ones who grow beards in the winter. But them Minnesotas got good fishing and can hold their liquor. Plus they got all them Swedes who ain't too smart, so's it's easy to sneak out on your bar tab at closing time.

I'm kinda agreeing with you on Norwegian. That's over by Europe, where they're always eating bran flakes and flicking their ponytails like supermodels.

But playing hockey is the best job in America. Hell, they even got a job called goon. All you do is play about five minutes a game, punch somebody out, then go sit down again. It's even better than being a bouncer cuz there's no college boys playing rap on the jukebox.

Now I'm asking you, Buford, where else can you get a job that offers free lumber, laundry and dental, you get a clubhouse with decent carpeting, and when you brawl the cops don't call your parole officer?

27

How to Keep From Getting Your Ass Kicked at Sports Bars in Wisconsin

Nothing causes bad luck faster than rooting for sissy teams. Guys see you at a sports bar, pounding wine coolers and yelling for a team of effeminate qualities, they got no choice but to take you out back and beat you with a cardboard Old Style display. It's Northern White Trash law.

Take the guy who shows up at a Stevens Point, Wisconsin bar with a Michael Irvin jersey on. First off, he ain't gonna get no chicks. Decent ladies know Dallas in Cambodian means, "I get my ass beat at arm-wrestling by bank tellers."

That's the bad luck I'm trying to clue you about.

There's basically three ways to avoid getting your ass kicked in a sports bar:

1. Don't root for nobody from the South

When people think white trash, they think South. Problem is, the white trash down there gives us a bad name. People be confusing us for them guys with no teeth who play banjos and look like their ma was a zoo animal.

But there's a big difference. Us northerners are more behaved. When we date our cousins, at least we take 'em out for dinner and buy 'em something pretty before we get to having babies.

But say the foreman sees you rooting for the Atlanta Braves. He'll figure you're from the South, which means you got the I.Q. of a belt sander. It also means he'll assign you to mopping up the hazardous waste room on account of you won't know better.

2. Don't root for fruities from Southern California

The guy gets home from work everyday at 6 p.m., slips out of his cute yellow sweater and his Dockers, cranks up some Yanni and sits on the couch, careful not to get crumples on his fuscia jogging suit.

"Honey," he says to his woman, "I had a hard day at the computer factory, lifting them heavy computer chips and all. Could you please get me a designer water with a lemon twist?"

That's why you don't root for nobody from Southern California. Next to France and Melrose Place, there ain't no place sissier.

Everybody in Southern California is either a advertising guy, a lawyer, a computer geek or has fake blonde hair and talks like he was in that movie *The Birdcage*. You ever see a guy from California chop a cord of wood with only an ax and a sixer of Pigs Eye?

Say you go to that bar in Stevens Point dressed like a Californian. You got your cell phone, your pager, your jogging suit and your cute little gel hair. The smart money says you get your ass whupped before you pound your first wine spritzer—even if there's only old men and cripples at the bar.

What happens the next day when you show up at the plant, and all the guys is wanting to know what happened? If you gotta say, "I was rooting too loud for the Lakers and got my ass whupped by a quadriplegic," expect to get reassigned to hazardous waste storage by noon.

3. But what if a South team is playing them sissies from Southern California?

Here's where the figuring gets hard. On one hand, you got your inbreds. On the other, you got fruities who'd rather be watching Barbra Streisand on pay-per-view.

So you go with the tie-breaker: which name sounds the manliest.

Say Duke is playing USC. Duke sounds like a bunch of tea-sipping fruities from England who got wigs and tights. "Cheeves, I seem to have misplaced my spectacles."

USC is named the Trojans, which used to be an army from Greece or someplace like that. Since armies is manlier than crossdressers, go with USC.

But that ain't true if you're watching, say, Florida-UCLA. This time, the southerners is named after a gator, which bites people and makes good cowboy boots.

The Southern Californians is named after a Bruin, which most people call bears. But if he was a real bear, he wouldn't be living in California cuz the only thing to eat in the garbage is tofu and low-fat yogurt. That's why they call him Bruin, which in bear language means, "I got an appointment with my hair stylist at 3."

But say you got the worst of all cases: The Anaheim Mighty Ducks is playing the Dallas Stars.

One team's named after a movie that didn't have no explosions. The other's named after some actresses who spend all their time in tanning booths and getting electrolysis.

At this point, slowly back away, turn off the TV, burn your clothes and take a hot shower. You don't want none of that getting contagious on you.

Teams That Will Jinx You So You Won't Even Be Able to Grow a Decent Beard, Like That Dainty Ethan Hawke

1. Alabama Crimson Tide

Named after red laundry soap. What happens when they get tackled and their pants get dirty? Does their moms come down and pull their ears?

2. Philadelphia Phillies

I like chicks just as much as the next guy, but I wouldn't name no baseball team after them. Next thing you know, a pitcher is getting shelled in the middle of the fourth inning, and the manager stops the game to talk about his feelings.

3. Georgia Tech Yellow Jackets

The only people who wear yellow jackets is Hollywood fruities and old ladies on Easter. If they're gonna have a sissified name, they should do it right and call themselves the Georgia Tech Boutonnieres, which is French for, "I got a flower stuck on my jacket."

4. Orlando Magic

Ain't this cute. Little fairies with batons prancing around putting spells on princesses. You think a fairy gonna go to the boards with Mutumbo?

5. Los Angeles Clippers

Only L.A. would name their team after a hairdresser.

The Five Manliest Teams

1. Minnesota Vikings

The manliest team of all, on account of they're named after guys who used to ride around in boats, kick the %$#@ outta Scotsmen for wearing dresses, and steal all their liquor and women.

2. Green Bay Packers

It ain't glamorous, but Northern White Trash who's been evicted a decent amount knows the value of a good packer. Especially if you don't got enough money for a U-Haul and got to fit everything in the skimpy-assed box of a Chevy S-10.

3. Colorado Buffaloes

Okay, so's they ain't much sport for hunting. But they're big, furry, and they got them ZZ Top beards. You can tell they're the union stewards of the Animal Kingdom by the way they stand around doing nothing.

4. Milwaukee Brewers

Makers of the sacred nectar. From what you call your religious perspective, they're probably the fifth most important deity in the Universe after God, Jesus, the Virgin Mother and bail bondsmen. Don't root for these guys and the smart money says St. Peter smokes your ass before you get a word in edgewise.

5. North Dakota Fighting Sioux

Named after guys who didn't have jobs and just rode around hunting and fighting for the hell of it. Think of 'em as the olden days' version of bikers, only they dressed like them guys from Pocahontas and didn't have to worry about burning oil in their horses. Pretty much figure any team with "fighting" in their name is gonna be manly— except for the Fighting Irish, who wear dresses and even get their ass kicked by England.

28

I Cheated on My Cousin & Killed My Uncle's Bird Dog

Dear Dr. Verne:

You gotta help me! I was at a family reunion at my Uncle Billy's place when it all happened. My cousin Marty caught me in the bedroom naked with his wife. She started it.

Anyway, while I was taking the gun away from him, it went off. The slug went through the floor of the trailer and killed my uncle's bird dog.

Now my wife is mad at me and I ain't getting any. Besides that, I ain't got $300 for no new bird dog. Everybody's mad at me. What should I do?

—*New Hampshire White Trash*

Dear New Hampshire Trash:

First off, fighting with your relatives is what separates us white trash from a lesser class of people, like what they got in Hollywood. When they fight with each other, they hire up some fruit boy lawyer with them oval-shaped glasses to throw paperwork at each other. Decent people, they try to shoot each other, on account of it's cheaper.

But I'd be thinking about getting some new lies when you get caught naked. Me, I never had much luck with the she-started-it excuse.

My first trick is to pretend I'm a doctor and I'm doing one of them mammograms. Since it's a big French word, husbands don't know what the hell you're talking about and will leave you alone.

But say you're dealing with a smarter than normal husband, like maybe he's a union steward or something. That means you go to stage two: Pretend like you didn't know she was married.

Of course, your cousin ain't gonna buy this, on account of you was at the wedding. But just tell him you was hammered that day, and that all white trash look alike, and you thought you was romping with your own woman. He's bound to cut you some slack, on account of this probably happened to him before.

This bird dog thing is a lot more serious though. Since you ain't got the 300, I'd try trading your uncle something of equal value, like your life-size pheasant statue that doubles as a cig lighter. But you gotta get on this quick, cuz killing a guy's bird dog is way more serious than messing with his wife.

29

YUPPIES ANONYMOUS:
A 12-STEP GUIDE TO RECTIFYING
YOUR SISSY WAYS

Now that you read this far—or got somebody to read it for you—you're finally realizing what it takes to live the wholesome Northern White Trash way.

Problem is, some of you is getting them feelings of inadequacy. You know you ain't lived right. You know you been sneaking Zimas and watching *Friends* with the shades drawn. And you're probably saying to yourself, "Thanks, Dr. Verne, for showing me that my life has fallen into a state of despair."

You're ready to amend your ways.

Nowadays, you get to blame this stuff on a disadvantaged childhood, which is the polite way of saying your folks sucked.

Maybe you was raised in some fruity subdivision with too many goddamned wind socks. Or maybe you wasn't privileged enough to shoot long arms out of a duck boat when you was young.

Don't worry. According to them modern sciences, going sissy, setting fire to the Junior Miss department at Kmart, or asking your grandpa's false teeth for a date to the prom, all that stuff gets blamed on disadvantaged childhoods these days. Don't ask me why. Just be thankful I'm giving you a good excuse here.

Problem is, them scientists ain't invented no dope to cure you. Which is why you need my 12-step program, Yuppies Anonymous.

As long as you're in a 12-step program, you get to say you're "recovering," which means chicks will have pity and won't get as mad when you paw at 'em. It offers you, the Volvo-driving fruity with the string on your sunglasses, the chance to do something about your sickness. I ain't saying you'll get dewussified. But at least the meetings got free coffee and lots of people to bum smokes from.

The Yuppies Anonymous 12-Step Tradition

1. I admit that I am powerless over brie and white wine and grinding my own coffee beans from some candy-ass Latin place nobody ever heard of, and that my life has become wussified.

2. I have come to believe that a power greater than me can restore me to sanity, so's I'll stop posing in the mirror trying to look like them guys from the Benetton ads.

3. I made the decision to turn my life over to the care of some decent Northern White Trash, who'll drown me in a flower pot if I even get to thinking about wearing plum-colored Dockers.

4. I made a searching and fearless moral inventory of myself. Okay, so I lied. But I got the idea on blocks in my front yard. I should be getting to it any day now.

5. I admitted to God, myself and another human being the exact nature of my wrongs—only I left out the part about the 16-year-old on that business trip to Boston. I swear she looked at least 22.

6. I am entirely ready to have God remove all these defects of character, even if He's gotta torture my ass with some dental equipment from the Nazis.

7. I humbly ask God to remove my shortcomings, so I can throw out them goddamned garbanzo beans and bee-line it to Old Country Buffet.

8. I made a list of all people I had harmed, and became willing to make amends to them all, except that old guy whose car I rammed at the hardware store last week. He shouldn't have parked so close.

9. I made direct amends to such people wherever possible, except if it was at the same time the Mariners-Royals was on satellite.

10. I continued to take a personal inventory and when I was wrong admitted it, just so it wasn't about that liquor store robbery on 13th Avenue last Tuesday. I got an alibi.

11. I sought through prayer, meditation and plenty of liquor to improve my conscious contact with the Northern White Trash, praying only for knowledge and a few extra bucks, seeing as how knowledge don't get you %$#@ if you're living out of a station wagon.

12. Having had a spiritual awakening as a result of these steps, I tried to carry this message to other yuppies,

so's they would owe me when they got cured and probably buy me beers.

30

THE INSENSITIVE MAN'S X-MAS SURVIVAL GUIDE

You're a man. Which means on the evolutionary scale, you're more advanced than a Chicago alderman, but way behind a pair of yellow hip waders.

Sure, you try to be sensitive. Like that time your kid was bawling cuz her guinea pig got ate by the German shepherd. You put you're arm around her all comforting like and said, "Hey, kid, what's with the tears? Hell, I was thinking about eating that rat anyways. Probably make a good snack with some mustard and barbecue sauce."

But you still caught hell. That's because men being sensitive is like Leonardo DiCaprio winning a lumberjack competition. It just ain't gonna happen.

Problem is, you got Christmas coming up. The worst season for men. It's the time we gotta reflect on the needs and wishes of others, which ain't our natural way.

But I also got some good news: They changed the rules of Christmas.

See, it used to be this celebration of Jesus, who they say was a damn good carpenter—even though he dressed like them fat ladies who stay in their gowns and watch TV all day. But then Jesus' in-laws grubbed on to the rights to X-mas and sold 'em to Wal-Mart.

Under the new Wal-Mart rules, they pretty much dropped all that caring and made it a time to get hammered, fight with your in-laws and go broke buying presents.

But you still gotta fake like you care. See, most women ain't aware of the new rules. They still want you to be sensitive, like that fruity Hugh Grant. Which is why I got this 5-point guide for faking your way through Christmas:

1. Avoid Household Appliances

Men is naturally attracted to these. They're large. They're shiny. They got engines. But women don't see appliances as what you call your expression of love—except if they're German. They'll get to figuring you view them as unpaid maids. Your true feelings will be exposed.

2. Avoid Power Tools

Chances are your woman never whispered in a moment of tenderness, "Honey, if you really love me, you'd score me that 9/16 inch chromium plated drill bit I always wanted." That's because women is weird; they don't understand the joy of hammering, sawing, puncturing and blow torching stuff. Fact is, giving your woman a radial arm saw or a rotary sander could get you're reproductive unit cut off or, worse, make her cut off your access to the remote control.

3. Resist the Old Bait & Switch

A lot of guys is powerless against the Bait & Switch Strategy. They're at Wal-Mart and there it is, a brand new Denver Nuggets sweatshirt or a pair of hunting pants in just your size. You know your woman ain't gonna score them for you. After all, women is always buying wuss stuff for Christmas, like sweaters with pictures of loons on 'em.

So you buy the sweatshirt and hunting pants for her, knowing they won't fit and you'll score 'em by default.

Problem is, we're men. We can outsmart kindergartners and bathroom fixtures, but not much else. Your woman will be on to you. And when you're protest by saying, "Honey, I always thought you looked like Demi Moore in size 38 camouflage pants," make sure there ain't loaded weapons nearby.

4. Think Volume

As a man, most of your brain is used for thinking about yourself. Fact is, outside eating and cable, there ain't much I.Q. left to consider anything else. That means you don't know what the hell your woman wants.

You can fix this by buying in volume. Instead of buying your woman one coat, buy eight in different colors. Chances are she won't like none of 'em, but she'll at least think you tried. You just happen to be pathetic.

Which is the great thing about women. They always cut slack for the pathetic. She'll expect less of you in the future, which is way better than having her like what you got her.

5. Buy Lots of Worthless Crap

Since men ain't got the mechanical requirements for an imagination, we usually go for worthless gifts. Like winter boots, clothesline poles, a rear-window defroster.

But don't expect your woman to turn to you on Christmas morning with moist eyes and say, "Oh, honey, new rain gutters!"

Most people want worthless stuff for Christmas. You know, like jewelry, fancy clothes, opera tickets and them assorted cheeses from LaCrosse. The goal is to give them junk they'd never buy.

That's because in America, the best way to show your love is to waste your money on someone else.

31

LESSONS ON WINNING BAR FIGHTS,
SCORING POINTS WITH THE BOSS'
WIFE, AND DRUNK DRIVING FOR THE
HOLIDAY SEASON

Most people figure Christmas parties is times of good
cheer. You're supposed to get together with co-workers,
celebrate fortunes, and be thankful you ain't a U.S. senator or recently got your hand mauled by a wolverine.

But to Northern White Trash, X-mas parties is pure
danger. If you never cheated on your husband or blowed
chow on the best shoes of the foreman's wife, this here's
your opportunity.

Which is why you need to show a little class this holiday season.

The Proper Ways of Dressing Up

Your woman gets pumped about the company X-mas
party. It's that one time of year she gets to wear the fancy
dress she got from Sears for your brother's fifth wedding

back in '93. So maybe she put on 10 or 20 pounds since then. Okay, maybe 50 if your stump grinding business is going well and you got extra money for Stovetop Stuffing.

But there ain't nothing finer than a woman in a tight black dress, even if she is your wife.

Problem is, that means you gotta dress up too. Try jaking outta this all you want, but your woman's gonna be pissed if you figure on wearing hunting clothes and a Chicago Bears hat.

Give in on this point. From where I'm sitting, you're gonna get in a lot bigger trouble as the night goes on.

Think about some nice flannel that got no blood on it from field dressing deers, maybe a Marlboro jacket, your best steel toes and your dress up Phillies hat—the one that got no bearing grease or sweat on it.

This, friends, is what you call class.

The Torture of Mingling

Mingling is the worst part of any X-mas party. In case you didn't know, mingling in Ojibwe means: "I'd rather eat a rich lady's china cupboard than yap with you."

When you first get there, everybody's acting like one big happy family, which they ain't, and that everybody cares about everybody, which they don't. That means you gotta mingle till you naturally separate into bosses, white collar guys and decent working people, at which point you can start getting hammered.

But be careful. This is the one time of year the boss acts human. That means he might talk to you.

He's gonna want to meet your woman, ask about the family, tell your wife how good of a worker you is, even though he only pays $7.40 an hour and thinks your name is Harry.

You also gotta make an impression on the boss' wife. A few tips for scoring in this situation: Try not to talk about fan belts, drinking the worms in tequila or the last burglary you did at that hair replacement clinic.

She being a rich lady and all, you gotta talk refined. Try saying some deep and thoughtful stuff like, "Utah ain't gonna be &%$# this year if Stockton don't start hitting the three," or "You know of any decent places for trout fishing around here?"

This is what you call subtle. Rich folks get impressed by that. Next thing you know, she'll be telling the old man how refined you is, you get promoted to foreman, and next X-mas you'll be scoring your woman a dress from some place really classy, like Ben Franklin.

Scoring at the Gift Exchange

There's usually some fruit in your company who wants to do a gift exchange. A good way of avoiding this: Lock her in your trunk till the party's over.

But if you already got two priors and you don't wanna be looking at a three strikes kidnapping charge, quit whining and take it.

You don't usually get no decent gifts outta this. Most people give stuff like polka-dotted ties so's they can laugh at you.

But at least *you* can be classy.

Me, I always wrap up a hockey stick. It's good for unclogging gutters, pushing your kids outta the way of the TV, or beating your neighbors who squawk about all the broke snowmobiles in your front yard. You can also use it to hold up vines in your tomato patch or hunt deer when you're too broke for ammo.

So while everybody else is giving dainty little pen sets or them paper weights—do these people work in a &%$#*&% wind tunnel or what?—you'll be the only guy showing class.

Danger! Open Bar Ahead!

Putting an open bar in front of white trash is like throwing a batch of naked cheerleaders into a prison exercise yard. You're in trouble. I ain't even gonna advise you on this on account of you'll be in a coma by morning, so's you won't be able to thank me. But I got some suggestions:

1.) Belly up to a crowded part of the bar. When you pass out, you'll land on someone first, instead of smacking your head on the floor too hard.

2.) If you gotta barf, do it with class. Never barf on the bar. Just bend down so no one sees, barf, then throw somebody's coat on top of it. Nobody's the wiser, and the bartender won't cut you off.

3.) Once you got about nine or fourteen shots in you, anything with two legs is gonna be looking fine. But don't go pawing at the waitress. This also gets you cut off. Make sure you paw at the wife of a buddy who's littler than you. Which leads us to...

Nothing Better Than a Good Brawl

According to section 4.32 of the Northern White Trash Constitution, "any party, wedding, funeral or holiday gathering must include at least one brawl. Cat fights or stomping parking lot attendants do not fulfill this requirement."

Which is why it's your sacred duty to do a little knuckling.

Just remember: It ain't your fault. It's the boss' for having that open bar. Moron shouldda knowed better.

It's a good idea to pick on little guys. Whiskey don't taste good if your mouth is bleeding. Little guys usually punch you in the stomach or neck, which don't cut into your drinking ability.

But make sure you win. If you get your ass whupped by the midget whose wife you was pawing at, most guys'll figure you're a cross-dresser or a Dodgers fan. So's if you're too hammered and might lose, fake like you're having a pancreas failure. Your buddies won't know what that is. They'll give you shots of Beam to make it better. And nobody'll punch you out for at least a year, on account of they don't wanna catch pancreas failure, too.

Bonus Round for the Ladies

Okay, ladies, so your old man has ignored you all night. Now he's back to pawing at the midget's wife. That means you got diplomatic immunity to do some tom catting yourself—and finally score a decent man.

My advice: Do the old Heaving Chest Maneuver on one of them front office guys.

Two things you need to know about white collar fruities: First off, they're part girl, so you gotta check to make sure they're capable of reproducting activity. Second off, they got the romantic powers of a smoked cod. But at least they're into that sensitive stuff, which means they'll think it's therapeutic if you talk about poisoning your husband with some Weed-B-Gone.

Of course, the front office guy's trophy wife is gonna be pissed. Don't worry. You could whup her two days from Hell on account of all she eats is Slimfast and celery. Besides, she'll be ascared you'll put bruises on her, which won't match her jogging suit when she's power walking at the mall.

When the trophy wife ain't looking, drag Mr. Fruity into a supply closet. Once he gets a taste of that good Northern Trash, he ain't going back.

And if he's gonna keep the affair going, he's gonna have to schedule your old man for overtime to get him outta the house. That puts you in the bonus round: You got an extra man on the side, and there's more overtime money for scoring Lean Cuisine.

The Best Way to Drunk Drive is in Someone Else's Car

Once it gets past ten, the bosses and the white collars usually go home, on account of they can't hold their liquor and gotta jog on their NordicTracks. Which means for the next few hours the decent working people got the bar to themself. Which means you can brawl, have domestic arguments and wreck stuff.

But sooner or later the dainty little %$#@ with the bowtie behind the bar, who's probably working his way through law school so's he can sue grandmas and orphans, is gonna call it closing time.

Enter your biggest problem of the night: drunk driving. Seeing as how your woman took the truck to meet Mr.

Sissified at the Holiday Inn, you either gotta walk it, hitch it, or catch a ride.

But the smart white trash knows there's another option. See, you figured the evening would go like this. You'd get hammered, your woman would get pissed, she'd take off with a white collar fruity, and you'd be stuck hoofing it. Which is why she drove your truck, and you borrowed your buddy's.

The best way to drunk drive is in someone else's car. Say you sideswipe a couple cars, or end up parking in the showroom of a pet store when you miss a turn. You're gonna be too hung in the morning to deal with it.

If a major accident happens, just abandon the truck, hitch a ride home, and tell your buddy it was stolen in the morning.

After all, he's your buddy, ain't he? He shouldn't mind giving of himself so the truly needy can sleep off an open bar.

Ain't that what X-mas is all about?

32

Locusts, Famine and Forty Years of Flatulence

Dear Dr. Verne:

Me and my buddy, Galen, we owns a drywalling business. A couple weeks ago we was hanging and mudding some rock on a remodel job in one of them strip malls in the suburbs.

In the strip mall was one of them wussy bars. Galen (he's a real bird dog) kept noticing these good looking yuppie chicks going into this wussy bar.

Now those yuppie chicks don't do nothing for me, but Galen says that all babes, even those yuppie babes, deserve to have a real man once in a while.

So one night after work Galen and I wandered down to the wussy bar only because I wanted to do what was right. Well, one of them yuppie babes got kinda friendly with me. We ended up back at her place and she got real friendly with me, if you know what I mean.

The next morning I woke up and smelled the worst smell I ever sniffed. I asked the yuppie babe what the hell was the smell. She said, "I just have a little flatulence."

Verne, I was real scared. I don't know what flatulence is. Now Galen, he's got a real smart son, Galen Jr., by either his second or third wife. Hell, Galen Jr. is so smart he almost got into the sheet metal apprentice program.

Anyways, Galen Jr. thinks that the flatulence may be one of them sexually transmitted diseases. Verne, should I quit worrying or should I soak something in kerosene?

—*Stan the Drywall Man,*
Providence, R.I.

Dear Stan:

I'm thinking this flatulence is one of them Bible things. Say too many people get to stealing and drinking and coveting thy neighbor's woman, which makes Moses pissed. So he orders up one of them 40 years of flatulence, which means floods and locusts and famine. That way people know not to &%$# with Moses.

I asked the barmaid at Johnny's Tavern if this was right. She said yeah. But she don't got figured why that yuppie babe was talking about locusts when her apartment got to stinking.

Me, I figure she was just trying to impress you with big words, seeing as how you got your own business and you'd probably take her to the Indian Casino every night if you was married.

But the barmaid, she figures that yuppie babe was worried about Moses putting 40 years of flatulence on her for sinning. If she was decent and God-fearing, He wouldda born her with spandex and bigger hair. But since she's taken to them Godless yuppie ways, she knows Moses'll be more ornery than a foreman who just got his child support jacked.

Next time you sees that yuppie babe, give her a five-gallon pail of Ortho. She gonna need it when them locusts show up.

About the Author

Dr. Verne Edstrom, Esq. is considered America's leading scholar on Northern White Trash culture.

He is a graduate of the Red Wing Boys Reformatory, thought by many to be the Harvard of the Minnesota juvenile corrections system. He later received a scholarship to Stillwater State Penitentiary, where he majored in pipe-fitting. After graduation, Dr. Verne went on to earn his doctorate from the prestigious Northern White Trash Studies Program at Bemidji State University.

As an acclaimed public speaker and consultant, Dr. Verne's services are in great demand. In the Clinton Administration, he served as a special envoy to France and Los Angeles to help those countries become less sissified. He conducts regular seminars on power tool theft for the Gambino Crime Family. And his annual three-day symposium, "How to Sneak Into America, Get Yourself a Disability Scam & Spend the Rest of Your Days Watching Cable & Pounding Grain Belt," was attended by more than 100,000 people in Mexico City last spring.

Dr. Verne also sits on the national boards of Yuppies Anonymous, the American Bookies Association and the Save the Manual Transmission Foundation.

He presently resides in Des Moines with his 8-10 children, where he serves as a columnist for *Cityview*.

Dr. Verne's Web site can be found at http://homestead.com/drverne.